HOW TO READ A FINANCIAL REPORT

HOW TO READ A

WRINGING VITAL SIGNS OUT OF

Eighth Edition

WILEY

FINANCIAL REPORT

THE NUMBERS

JOHN A. TRACY AND TAGE C. TRACY

Cover Design: Wiley
Cover Illustration: Wiley

Published by John Wiley & Sons, Inc., Hoboken, New Jersey.

The Seventh Edition of How to Read a Financial Report: Wringing Vital Signs Out of the Numbers was published by John Wiley & Sons, Inc, in 2009.

Published simultaneously in Canada.

For general information on our other products and services or for technical support, please contact our Customer Care Department within the United States at (800) 762-2974, outside the United States at (317) 572-3993 or fax (317) 572-4002.

Wiley publishes in a variety of print and electronic formats and by print-on-demand. Some material included with standard print versions of this book may not be included in e-books or in print-on-demand. If this book refers to media such as a CD or DVD that is not included in the version you purchased, you may download this material at http://booksupport.wiley.com. For more information about Wiley products, visit www.wiley.com.

Library of Congress Cataloging-in-Publication Data:

Tracy, John A.
    How to read a financial report: wringing vital signs out of the numbers / John A. Tracy, CPA, Tage Tracy. — 8th ed.
        pages   cm
    Includes index.
        ISBN 978-1-118-73584-8 (pbk.); ISBN 978-1-118-73558-9 (ebk); ISBN 978-1-118-73592-3 (ebk)
    1. Financial statements.   I. Tracy, Tage C.   II. Title.
    HF5681.B2T733   2014
    657'.3—dc23
                                                                        2013035597

Printed in the United States of America

10 9 8 7 6 5

CONTENTS

LIST OF EXHIBITS

PREFACE TO THE EIGHTH EDITION

When I started this book my new co-author on this edition, my son Tage, was entering his senior year of high school. Today he is a successful business and financial consultant in San Diego. Truth be known, he writes better than his old man. So, it is with great personal pleasure and pride that I welcome my son Tage as co-author on this edition. He's a chip off the old block. In case you're wondering about his name, it is Swedish and Danish in origin.

At the time the first edition was released in 1980, the Dow Jones Industrial Average hovered around 850 (really!). This most-watched stock market index reached 11,700 in early 2000, and then it abruptly plunged, causing a big dent in my retirement savings. The Dow recovered over the following years, but then dropped again. As I write this sentence the Dow is about 15,000. As J. P. Morgan once said, "The market will fluctuate." Millions of individuals keep their money in the stock market, and stock investments are a large part of most retirement plans. Knowing how to read a financial report is as important as ever.

This edition catches up with the major changes in financial reporting since the previous edition. At the top of this list is the movement toward different financial reporting standards for private and small businesses. At the same time, the basic architecture of the book remains unchanged. The framework of the book has proved very successful for more than 33 years. I'd be a fool to mess with this success formula. My mother did not raise a fool. Cash flows are underscored throughout the book. This cash flow emphasis is the hallmark of the book.

I prepared all the exhibits in the book as Excel worksheets. To request a copy of the workbook file of all the exhibits, please contact me at my e-mail address: tracyj@colorado.edu. I express my sincere thanks to all of you who have sent compliments about my book. The royalties from sales of the book are nice, but the bouquets from readers are icing on the cake.

Not many books of this ilk make it to the eighth edition. It takes a good working partnership between the author and the publisher. I thank most sincerely the many persons at John Wiley & Sons who have worked with me on the book for more than three decades now. The suggestions on my first draft of the book by Joe Ross, then national training director of Merrill Lynch, were extraordinarily helpful. The continuing support of Debra Englander over the years is very much appreciated. And I'd be remiss without mentioning Tula Batanchiev and Judy Howarth, who have been a pleasure to work with on this edition. They have made the new edition much better than if we had been left on our own. Books are the collaboration of good editors and good authors. We had good editors; you'll have to be the judge how good the authors are.

I rededicate this book to Gordon B. Laing, my original editor and sponsor of the book. His superb editing was a blessing that few authors enjoy. His guidance, encouragement, and enthusiasm made all the difference. He was a true gentleman who taught me a great deal about writing. His criticisms of my manuscript drafts were sharp but always kindly and supportive. Gordon took much pride in the success of the book—as well he should have! Gordon has passed but I'd like to say again that I couldn't have done it without him.

JOHN A. TRACY

Boulder, Colorado
August, 2013

Part One

FUNDAMENTALS

1

STARTING WITH CASH FLOWS

Cash Flows Summary for a Business

Savvy business managers, lenders, and investors pay a lot of attention to *cash flows*. Cash inflows and outflows are the heartbeat of every business. Without a steady heartbeat of cash flows, a business would soon have to go on life support, or die.

So, we start with cash flows. For our example we use a business that has been operating many years. This established business makes profit regularly and, equally important, it keeps in good financial condition. It has a good credit history, and banks lend money to the business on competitive terms. Its present stockholders would be willing to invest additional capital in the business, if needed. None of this comes easy. It takes good management to make profit consistently, to secure capital, and to stay out of financial trouble. Many businesses fail these imperatives, especially when the going gets tough.

Exhibit 1.1 summarizes the company's cash inflows and outflows for the year just ended, and shows two separate groups of cash flows. First are the cash flows of its profit-making activities—cash inflows from sales and cash outflows for expenses. Second are the other cash inflows and outflows of the business—raising capital, investing capital in assets, and distributing some of its profit to shareowners.

We assume you're fairly familiar with the cash inflows and outflows listed in Exhibit 1.1. Therefore, we are brief in describing the cash flows at this early point in the book:

- The business received $51,680,000 during the year from selling products to its customers. It should be no surprise that this is its largest source of cash inflow. Cash inflow from sales revenue is needed for paying expenses. During the year the company paid $34,760,000 for the products it sells to customers. And, it had sizable cash outflows for operating expenses, interest on its debt (borrowed money), and income tax. The net result of its cash flows of profit-making activities is a $3,105,000 cash increase for the year—an extremely important number that managers, lenders, and investors watch closely.

- Moving on to the second group of cash flows during the year, the business increased the amount borrowed on notes payable $625,000, and its stockholders invested an additional $175,000 in the business. Together these two external sources of capital provided $800,000, which is in addition to the internal $3,105,000 cash from its profit-making activities during the year. On the other side of the ledger, the business spent $3,625,000 for building improvements, for new machines and equipment, and for intangible assets. Finally, the business distributed $750,000 cash to its stockholders from profit. This distribution from profit is included in the second group of cash flows. In other words, the $3,105,000 cash flow from profit is before the distribution to shareowners.

- The net result of all cash inflows and outflows is a $470,000 cash *decrease* during the year. Don't jump to any conclusions; the net decrease in cash in and of itself is neither good nor bad. You need more information than just the summary of cash flows to come to any conclusions about the financial performance and situation of the business.

EXHIBIT 1.1—SUMMARY OF CASH FLOWS DURING YEAR
Dollar Amounts in Thousands

Cash Flows of Profit-Making Activities	
From sales of products to customers, which includes some sales made last year	$ 51,680
For acquiring products that were sold, or are still being held for future sale	$(34,760)
For operating expenses, some of which were incurred last year	$(11,630)
For interest on short-term and long-term debt, some of which applies to last year	$ (520)
For income tax, some of which was paid on last year's taxable income	$ (1,665)
Cash flow from profit-making activities during year	$ 3,105
Other Sources and Uses of Cash	
From increasing amount borrowed on interest-bearing notes payable	$ 625
From issuing additional capital stock (ownership shares) in the business	$ 175
For building improvements, new machines, new equipment, and intangible assets	$ (3,625)
For distributions to stockholders from profit	$ (750)
Net cash decrease from other sources and uses of cash	$ (3,575)
Net cash increase (decrease) during year	$ (470)

What Does Cash Flows Summary *Not* Tell You?

In Exhibit 1.1 we see that cash, the all-important lubricant of business activity, decreased $470,000 during the year. In other words, the total of cash outflows exceeded the total of cash inflows by this amount for the year. The cash decrease and the reasons for the decrease are important information. The cash flows summary tells an important part of the story of the business. But, cash flows do not tell the whole story. Business managers, investors in a business, business lenders, and many others need to know two other types of information about a business that are *not* reported in its cash flows summary.

The two most important types of information that a summary of cash flows does not tell you are:

1. The profit earned (or *loss* suffered) by the business for the period.

2. The financial condition of the business at the end of the period.

Now hold on. Didn't we just see in Exhibit 1.1 that the net cash increase from sales revenue less expenses was $3,105,000 for the year? You may ask: "Doesn't this cash increase equal the amount of profit earned for the year?" No, it doesn't. The net cash flow from profit-making operations during the year does not equal the amount of profit earned for the year. In fact, it's not unusual that these two numbers are very different.

Profit is an *accounting-determined* number that requires much more than simply keeping track of cash flows. The differences between using a checkbook to measure profit and using accounting methods to measure profit are important to understand. Hardly ever are cash flows during a period the correct amounts for measuring a company's sales revenue and expenses for that period. Summing up, profit cannot be determined from cash flows.

Furthermore, a summary of cash flows reveals virtually nothing about the *financial condition* of the business. Financial condition refers to the assets of the business matched against its liabilities at the end of the period. For example: How much cash does the company have in its checking account(s) at the end of the year? From the summary of cash flows (Exhibit 1.1) we see that the business decreased its cash balance $470,000 during the year. But we can't tell from the cash flows summary the company's ending cash balance. And, more importantly, the cash flows summary does not report the amounts of assets and liabilities of the business at the end of the period.

Profit Cannot Be Measured by Cash Flows

The company in this example sells products on *credit*. The business offers its customers a short period of time to pay for their purchases. Most of the company's sales are to other businesses, which demand credit. (In contrast, most retailers selling to individuals accept credit cards instead of extending credit to their customers.) In this example the company collected $51,680,000 from its customers during the year. However, some of this cash inflow was for sales made in the *previous* year. And, some sales made on credit in the year just ended had not been collected by the end of the year.

At year-end the company had *receivables* from sales made to its customers during the latter part of the year. These receivables will be collected early next year. Because some cash was collected from last year's sales and some cash was not collected from sales made in the year just ended, the total amount of cash collections during the year differs from the amount of *sales revenue* for the year.

Cash disbursements during the year are *not* the correct amounts for measuring expenses. The company paid $34,760,000 for products that are sold to customers (see Exhibit 1.1). At year-end, however, many products were still being held in *inventory*. These products had not yet been sold by year-end. Only the cost of products sold and delivered to customers during the year should be deducted as expense from sales revenue to measure profit. Don't you agree?

Furthermore, some of the company's product costs had not yet been paid by the end of the year. The company buys on credit and takes several weeks before paying its bills. The company has *liabilities* at year-end for recent product purchases and for operating costs as well.

Its cash payments during the year for operating expenses, as well as for interest and income tax expenses, are not the correct amounts to measure profit for the year. The company has liabilities at the end of the year for *unpaid expenses*. The cash outflow amounts shown in Exhibit 1.1 do not include the amounts of unpaid expenses at the end of the year.

In short, cash flows from sales revenue and for expenses are not the correct amounts for measuring profit for a period of time. Cash flows take place too late or too early for correctly measuring profit for a period. Correct timing is needed to record sales revenue and expenses in the right period.

The correct timing of recording sales revenue and expenses is called *accrual-basis accounting*. Accrual-basis accounting recognizes receivables from making sales on credit and recognizes liabilities for unpaid expenses in order to determine the correct profit measure for the period. Accrual-basis accounting also is necessary to determine the financial condition of a business—to record the assets and liabilities of the business.

Cash Flows Do Not Reveal Financial Condition

The cash flows summary for the year (Exhibit 1.1) does not reveal the financial condition of the company. Managers certainly need to know which assets the business owns and the amounts of each asset, including cash, receivables, inventory, and all other assets. Also, they need to know which liabilities the company owes and the amounts of each.

Business managers have the responsibility for keeping the company in a position to pay its liabilities when they come due to keep the business *solvent* (able to pay its liabilities on time). Business managers also have to keep the business *liquid* (having enough available cash when you need it). Furthermore, managers have to know whether assets are too large (or too small) relative to the sales volume of the business. Its lenders and investors want to know the same things about a business.

In brief, both the managers inside the business and lenders and investors outside the business need a summary of a company's financial condition (its assets and liabilities). They need a profit performance report as well, which summarizes the company's sales revenue and expenses and its profit for the year.

A cash flows summary is useful. In fact, a slightly different version of Exhibit 1.1 is one of the three primary financial statements reported by every business, but in no sense does the cash flows report take the place of the profit performance report and the financial condition report. The next chapter introduces these two financial statements, and shows the generally accepted format of a summary of cash flows (instead of the informal format shown in Exhibit 1.1).

A Final Note before Moving On

Over the past century (and longer) a recognized profession has developed, one of whose main functions is to prepare and report business financial statements—the *accounting profession*. A primary goal of the accounting profession has been to develop and enforce accounting and financial reporting standards that apply to all businesses. In other words, there is a "rule book" that businesses should obey in accounting for profit and in reporting profit, financial condition, and cash flows. Businesses are not free to make up their own individual accounting methods and financial reporting practices. The established rules and standards are collectively referred to as *generally accepted accounting principles* (GAAP). But things are getting more complicated these days, that's for sure.

In the United States there are serious beginnings to adopt separate rules for private companies versus public companies, and for small companies versus larger companies. Furthermore, the efforts to develop international accounting and financial reporting standards keep slogging along, with mixed results so far. We say more about the changing landscape of accounting and financial reporting standards in Chapter 23.

2

THREE FINANCIAL STATEMENTS

Reporting Financial Condition, Profit Performance, and Cash Flows

Business managers, lenders, and investors need to know the *financial condition* of a business. For this purpose they need a report that summarizes its assets and liabilities, as well as the ownership interests in the residual of assets in excess of liabilities. And they need to know the *profit* (or *loss*) *performance* of the business. They need a report that summarizes sales revenue and expenses for the most recent period and the resulting profit or loss. And, they need a summary of its *cash flows* for the period. Therefore, these three types of financial information are reported regularly by businesses to their managers, lenders, and investors.

Financial condition is communicated in an accounting report called the *balance sheet*, and profit activities are presented in an accounting report called the *income statement*. Cash flows are communicated in the *statement of cash flows*. Alternative titles for the balance sheet include "statement of financial condition" or "statement of financial position." An income statement may be titled "statement of operations" or "earnings statement." We stick with the names *balance sheet* and *income statement* to be consistent throughout the book. The statement of cash flows is almost always called just that.

The term *financial statements*, in the plural, generally refers to a complete set that includes a balance sheet, an income statement, and a statement of cash flows. Informally, financial statements are called just "financials." In almost all cases the financial statements

need to be supplemented with additional information, which is presented in *footnotes* and *supporting schedules*. One supporting schedule is very common—the *statement of changes in stockholders' (owners') equity*. The broader term *financial report* refers to all this, plus any additional commentary from management, narrative explanations, graphics, and promotional content that accompany the financial statements and their footnotes and supporting schedules.

The three financial statements for the company example introduced in Chapter 1 are now presented here in Exhibits 2.1, 2.2, and 2.3. The format and content of these three financial statements apply to manufacturers, wholesalers, and retailers—businesses that make or buy *products* that are sold to their customers. Although the financial statements of service businesses that don't sell products differ somewhat, Exhibits 2.1, 2.2, and 2.3 illustrate the basic framework and content of balance sheets, income statements, and statements of cash flows for all businesses.

Side notes: The term *profit* is not popular in income statements (or elsewhere in financial reports), so not many companies use the term (although some do). Profit comes across to many people as greedy or mercenary. The term suggests an excess or a surplus over and above what's necessary. You may hear the term *profit & loss* or *P&L statement* for the income statement. But this title is not used in external financial reports released outside a business.

EXHIBIT 2.1 – YEAR-END BALANCE SHEET

Dollar Amounts in Thousands

	Last Year	This Year	Change		Last year	This Year	Change
Cash	$ 3,735	$ 3,265	$ (470)	Accounts Payable	$ 2,675	$ 3,320	$ 645
Accounts Receivable	4,680	5,000	320	Accrued Expenses Payable	1,035	1,515	480
Inventory	7, 515	8,450	935	Income Tax Payable	82	165	83
Prepaid Expenses	685	960	275	Short-Term Notes Payable	3,000	3,125	125
Current Assets	$ 16,615	$ 17,675		**Current Liabilities**	$ 6,792	$ 8,125	
Property, Plant, and Equipment	$ 13,450	$ 16,500	3,050	**Long-Term Notes Payable**	$ 3,750	$ 4,250	500
Accumulated Depreciation	(3,465)	(4,250)	(785)				
Cost Less Depreciation	9,985	$ 12,250		Capital Stock–793,000 shares and 800,000 shares respectively	$ 7,950	$ 8,125	175
Intangible Assets	$ 5,000	$ 5,575	575	Retained Earnings	13,108	15,000	1,892
Long-Term Operating Assets	$ 14,985	$ 17,825		**Stockholders' Equity**	$ 21,058	$ 23,125	
				Total Liabilities and Stockholders'			
Total Assets	$ 31,600	$ 35,500	$ 3,900	**Equity**	$ 31,600	$ 35,500	$ 3,900

EXHIBIT 2.2—INCOME STATEMENT FOR YEAR
Dollar Amounts in Thousands

Sales Revenue	$ 52,000
Cost of Goods Sold Expense	(33,800)
Gross Margin	$ 18,200
Expenses	(12,480)
Depreciation Expense	(785)
Earnings before Interest and Income Tax	$ 4,935
Interest Expense	(545)
Earnings before Income Tax	$ 4,390
Income Tax Expense	(1,748)
Net Income	$ 2,642

Many businesses present a two-year comparative income statement and statement of cash flows, either because they legally have to or they decide to do so. In this chapter we don't need the previous year's information in these two statements. So, to keep it simple we do not include this information. In contrast, we need the previous year-end amounts in the balance sheet. Accordingly, the balance sheet in Exhibit 2.1 includes last year's amounts (as well as changes during the year).

EXHIBIT 2.3—STATEMENT OF CASH FLOWS FOR YEAR
Dollar Amounts in Thousands

Cash Flow from Operating Activities		
Net Income (from Income Statement)	$ 2,642	
Accounts Receivable Increase	(320)	
Inventory Increase	(935)	
Prepaid Expenses Increase	(275)	
Depreciation Expense	785	
Accounts Payable Increase	645	
Accrued Expenses Payable Increase	480	
Income Tax Payable Increase	83	$ 3,105
Cash Flow from Investing Activities		
Expenditures for Property, Plant, and Equipment	$ (3,050)	
Expenditures for Intangible Assets	(575)	(3,625)
Cash Flow from Financing Activities		
Increase in Short-Term Debt	$ 125	
Increase in Long-Term Debt	500	
Issuance of Additional Capital Stock Share	175	
Distribution of Cash Dividends from Profit	(750)	50
Decrease in Cash During Year		$ (470)
Cash Balance at Start of Year		3,735
Cash Balance at End of Year		$ 3,265

Income Statement

The first question on everyone's mind usually is whether a business made a profit or suffered a loss and how much. We start with the income statement and then move on to the balance sheet and statement of cash flows. The income statement summarizes sales revenue and expenses for a period of time—one year in Exhibit 2.2. All the dollar amounts reported in this financial statement are cumulative totals for the whole period.

The top line is the total amount of proceeds or gross income from sales to customers, and is generally called *sales revenue*. The bottom line is called *net income* (also net earnings, but seldom profit or net profit). Net income is the final profit after all expenses are deducted from sales revenue. The business in this example earned $2,642,000 net income on its sales revenue of $52,000,000 for the year; only a smidgeon more than 5 percent of its sales revenue remained as final profit (net income) after deducting all expenses.

The income statement is read in a step-down manner, like walking down stairs. Each step down is a deduction of one or more expenses. The first step deducts the cost of goods (products) sold from the sales revenue of goods sold, which gives *gross margin* (also called *gross profit*—one of the few instances of using the term *profit* in income statements). This measure of profit is called *gross* because many other expenses are not yet deducted.

Next, the broad category of operating expenses called *selling*, *general*, and *administrative expenses* and the depreciation expense (a

unique expense) are deducted from gross margin, giving *earnings before interest and income tax*. This measure of profit is also called *operating earnings*, or a similar title. Next, interest expense on debt is deducted, which gives earnings before income tax. The last step is to deduct income tax expense, which gives net income, the bottom line in the income statement.

Instead of the multiple-step income statement shown in Exhibit 2.2, which has three intermediate measures of profit, you may see a single-step income statement that reports only the final line of net income, which is shown in Exhibit 2.4.

EXHIBIT 2.4—SINGLE STEP INCOME STATEMENT
Dollar Amounts in Thousands

Sales Revenue	$ 52,000
Cost of Goods Sold	$ (33,800)
Selling, General, and Administrative Expenses	$ (12,480)
Depreciation Expense	$ (785)
Interest Expense	$ (545)
Income Tax Expense	$ (1,748)
Net Income	$ 2,642

Publicly owned business corporations are required to report *earnings per share* (EPS), which basically is annual net income divided by the number of capital stock shares. Privately owned businesses don't have to report EPS, but this figure may be useful to their stockholders. We explain earnings per share in Chapters 13 and 18.

In our income statement example (Exhibit 2.2) you see five different expenses. You may find more expense lines in an income statement, but seldom more than 10 or so as a general rule (unless the business had a very unusual year). Companies selling products are required to report their cost of goods sold expense. Some companies do not report depreciation expense on on a separate line in their income statements. However, depreciation is such a unique expense that we prefer to keep it separate from the other expenses.

Other than depreciation, Exhibit 2.2 includes just one broad, all-inclusive operating expenses line—"Selling, General, and Administrative Expenses." However, a business has the option of disclosing two or more operating expenses, and many do. Marketing, promotional, and selling expenses often are separated from general and administration expenses. The level of detail for expenses in income statements is flexible; financial reporting standards are somewhat loose on this point.

The sales revenue and expenses reported in income statements follow generally accepted conventions, which we briefly summarize here:

- **Sales Revenue:** The total amount received or to be received from the sales of products (and/or services) to customers during the period. Sales revenue is *net*, which means that discounts off list prices, prompt payment discounts, sales returns, and any other deductions from original sales prices are deducted to determine the sales revenue amount for the period. Sales taxes are not included in sales revenue, nor are excise taxes that might apply. In short, sales revenue is the amount the business should receive to cover its expenses and to provide profit (bottom-line net income).

- **Cost of Goods Sold Expense:** The total cost of goods (products) sold to customers during the period. This is clear enough. What might not be so clear, however, concerns goods that were shoplifted or are otherwise missing, as well as write-downs due to damage and obsolescence. The cost of such *inventory shrinkage* may be included in cost of goods sold expense for the year (or, this cost may be put in another expense account instead).

- **Selling, General, and Administrative Expenses (Operating Expenses):** Broadly speaking, every expense other than cost of goods sold, interest, and income tax. This broad category is a catchall for every expense not reported separately. In our example, depreciation is broken out as separate expense instead of being included with other operating expenses. Some companies report advertising and marketing costs separately from administrative and general costs, and some report research and development expenses separately. There are hundreds, even thousands, of specific operating expenses, some rather large and some very small. They range from salaries and wages of employees (large) to legal fees (small, one hopes).

- **Depreciation Expense:** The portions of original costs of long-term assets including buildings, machinery, equipment, tools, furniture, computers, and vehicles that is recorded to expense in one period. Depreciation is the "charge" for using these so-called fixed assets during the period. None of this expense amount is a cash outlay in the period recorded, which makes it a unique expense compared with other operating expenses.

- ***Interest Expense:*** The amount of interest on debt (interest-bearing liabilities) for the period. Other types of financing charges may also be included, such as loan origination fees.

- ***Income Tax Expense:*** The total amount due the government (both federal and state) on the amount of taxable income of the business during the period. Taxable income is multiplied by the appropriate tax rates. The income tax expense does not include other types of taxes, such as unemployment and Social Security taxes on the company's payroll. These other, nonincome taxes are included in operating expenses.

Balance Sheet

The balance sheet shown in Exhibit 2.1 follows the standardized format regarding the classification and ordering of assets, liabilities, and ownership interests in the business. Financial institutions, public utilities, railroads, and other specialized businesses use somewhat different balance sheet layouts. However, manufacturers and retailers, as well as the large majority of various types of businesses, follow the format presented in Exhibit 2.1.

On the left side the balance sheet lists *assets*. On the right side the balance sheet first lists the *liabilities* of the business, which have a higher-order claim on the assets. The sources of ownership (equity) capital in the business are presented below the liabilities, to emphasize that the owners or equity holders in a business (the stockholders of a business corporation) have a secondary and lower order claim on the assets—after its liabilities are satisfied.

Each separate asset, liability, and stockholders' equity reported in a balance sheet is called an *account*. Every account has a name (title) and a dollar amount, which is called its *balance*. For instance, from Exhibit 2.1 at the end of the most recent year:

Name of Account	Amount (Balance) of Account
Inventory	$8,450,000

The other dollar amounts in the balance sheet are either subtotals or totals of account balances. For example, the $17,675,000 amount for "Current Assets" at the end of this year does not represent an account but rather the subtotal of the four accounts making up this group of accounts. A line is drawn above a subtotal or total, indicating account balances are being added.

A double underline (such as for "Total Assets") indicates the last amount in a column. Notice also the double underline below "Net Income" in the income statement (Exhibit 2.2), indicating it is the last number in the column. (Some businesses do not put a double underline under net income.)

A balance sheet is prepared at the close of business on the last day of the income statement period. For example, if the income statement is for the year ending June 30, 2014, the balance sheet is prepared at midnight June 30, 2014. The amounts reported in the balance sheet are the balances of the accounts at that precise moment in time. The financial condition of the business is frozen for one split second. A business should be careful to make a precise and accurate cutoff to separate transactions between the period just ended and next period.

A balance sheet does not report the flows of activities in the company's assets, liabilities, and shareowners' equity accounts during the period. Only the ending balances at the moment the balance sheet is prepared are reported for the accounts. For example, the company reports an ending cash balance of $3,265,000 at the end of its most recent year (see Exhibit 2.1). Can you tell the total cash inflows and outflows for the year? No, not from the balance sheet; you can't even get a clue from the balance sheet alone.

A balance sheet can be presented in the landscape (horizontal) layout mode (as shown in Exhibit 2.1) or in the portrait (vertical) layout. The accounts reported in the balance sheet are not thrown together haphazardly in no particular order. According to long-standing rules, balance sheet accounts are subdivided into the following classes, or basic groups, in the following order of presentation:

Left Side (or Top Section)	*Right Side (or Bottom Section)*
Current assets	Current liabilities
Long-term operating assets	Long-term liabilities
Other assets	Owners' equity

Current assets are cash and other assets that will be converted into cash during one *operating cycle*. The operating cycle refers to the sequence of buying or manufacturing products, holding the products until sale, selling the products, waiting to collect the receivables from the sales, and finally receiving cash from customers. This sequence is the most basic rhythm of a company's operations; it is repeated over and over. The operating cycle may be short, only 60 days or less, or it may be relatively long, taking 180 days or more.

Assets not directly required in the operating cycle, such as marketable securities held as temporary investments or short-term loans made to employees, are included in the current assets class if they will be converted into cash during the coming year. A business pays in advance for some costs of operations that will not be charged to expense until next period. These *prepaid* expenses are included in current assets, as you see in Exhibit 2.1.

The second group of assets is labeled *Long-Term Operating Assets* in the balance sheet. These assets are not held for sale to customers; rather, they are used in the operations of the business. Broadly speaking, these assets fall into two groups: *tangible* and *intangible* assets. Tangible assets have physical existence, such as machines and buildings. Intangible assets do not have physical

existence, but they are legally protected rights (such as patents and trademarks), or they are such things as secret processes and well-known favorable reputations that give businesses important competitive advantages. Generally intangible assets are recorded only when the assets are purchased from a source outside the business.

The tangible assets of the business are reported in the "Property, Plant, and Equipment" account—see Exhibit 2.1 again. More informally, these assets are called *fixed assets*, although this term is generally not used in balance sheets. The word *fixed* is a little strong; these assets are not really fixed or permanent, except for the land owned by a business. More accurately, these assets are the long-term operating resources used over several years—such as buildings, machinery, equipment, trucks, forklifts, furniture, computers, and telephones.

The cost of a fixed asset—with the exception of land—is gradually charged off to expense over its useful life. Each period of use thereby bears its share of the total cost of each fixed asset. This apportionment of the cost of fixed assets over their useful lives is called *depreciation*. The amount of depreciation for one year is reported as an expense in the income statement (see Exhibit 2.2). The cumulative amount that has been recorded as depreciation expense since the date of acquisition up to the balance sheet date is reported in the *accumulated depreciation* account in the balance sheet (see Exhibit 2.1). As you see, the balance in the accumulated depreciation account is deducted from the original cost of the fixed assets.

In the example, the business owns various intangible long-term operating assets. These assets report the cost of acquisition. The cost of an intangible asset remains on the books until the business determines that the asset has lost value or no longer has economic benefit. At that time the business writes down (or writes off) the original cost of the intangible asset and charges the amount to an expense, usually *amortization expense*. Until recently, the general practice was to allocate the cost of intangible assets over arbitrary time periods. However, many intangible assets have indefinite and indeterminable useful lives. The conventional wisdom now is that it's better to wait until an intangible asset has lost value, at which time an expense is recorded.

You may see an account called "Other Assets" on a balance sheet, which is a catchall title for those assets that don't fit in the current assets or long-term operating assets classes. The company in this example does not have any such "other" assets.

The accounts reported in the *current liabilities* class are short-term liabilities that for the most part depend on the conversion of current assets into cash for their payment. Also, debts (borrowed money) that will come due within one year from the balance sheet date are put in this group. In our example, there are four accounts in current liabilities (see Exhibit 2.1 again). We explain these different types of current liabilities in later chapters.

Long-term liabilities (labeled *Long-Term Notes Payable* in Exhibit 2.1) are those whose maturity dates are more than one year after the balance sheet date. There's only one such account in our example. Either in the balance sheet or in a footnote, the maturity dates, interest rates, and other relevant provisions of long-term liabilities are disclosed.

Note: To simplify, we do not include footnotes with our financial statements example. We discuss footnotes in Chapter 17.

Liabilities are claims on the assets of a business; cash or other assets that will be later converted into cash will be used to pay the liabilities. (Also, cash generated by future profit earned by the business will be available to pay its liabilities.) Clearly, all liabilities of a business should be reported in its balance sheet to give a complete picture of the financial condition of a business.

Liabilities are also sources of assets. For example, cash increases when a business borrows money. Inventory increases when a business buys products on credit and incurs a liability that will be paid later. Also, typically a business has liabilities for unpaid expenses and has not yet used cash to pay these liabilities. Another reason for reporting liabilities in the balance sheet is to account for the sources of the company's assets—to answer the question: Where did the company's total assets come from?

Some part of the total assets of a business comes not from liabilities but from its owners investing capital in the business and from retaining some or all of the profit the business earns that is not distributed to its owners. In this example the business is organized legally as a corporation. Its *stockholders' equity* accounts in the balance sheet reveal the sources of the company's total assets in excess of its total liabilities. Notice in Exhibit 2.1 the two stockholders' (owners') equity sources, which are called *capital stock* and *retained earnings*.

When owners (stockholders of a business corporation) invest capital in the business, the capital stock account is increased.* Net income earned by a business less the amount distributed to owners increases the retained earnings account. The nature of retained earnings can be confusing; therefore, we explain this account in depth at the appropriate places in the book. Just a quick word of advice here: Retained earnings is *not*—we repeat, is *not*—an asset. Get such a notion out of your head.

———————————

*Many business corporations issue *par value* stock shares. The shares have to be issued for a certain minimum amount, called the par value, but the corporation may issue the shares for more than par value. The excess over par value is put in a second account called "Paid-In Capital in Excess of Par Value." This is not shown in the balance sheet example, because the separation between the two accounts has little practical significance for financial reporting.

Statement of Cash Flows

Exhibit 2.3 presents the company's statement of cash flows for the same year as its income statement (Exhibit 2.2). The balance sheets at the start and end of the year can be thought of as the bookends of the company's two activity statements—the income statement and the cash flows statement. The two activity statements reveal the reasons for the changes in the company's financial condition from the start of the year to the end of the year.

We explain the statement of cash flows extensively in Chapters 14 and 15. At this point we simply introduce this financial statement. If you compare the informal summary of cash flows presented in Chapter 1 (Exhibit 1.1) with the formal statement of cash flows in this chapter (Exhibit 2.3), you would see several differences.

You might think that the financial statement that summarizes cash flows would be fairly simple and straightforward. But we regret to tell you that the statement of cash flows is more complicated than meets the eye. To understand cash flows you first should have a basic understanding of profit accounting, which we explain in Chapter 3. And you should have a good grasp on the how the three financial statements are interconnected, which we explain in Chapter 4. None of this is explained in financial reports. Financial statements do not come with a cheat sheet. In preparing financial statements accountants presume that you know these things—which if you don't mind us saying so is damn presumptuous of them.

3

PROFIT ACCOUNTING

An Important Question

In Chapter 2 we introduce the three primary financial statements for a representative business example. See Exhibits 2.1 (balance sheet), 2.2 (income statement), and 2.3 (statement of cash flows). These three financial statements provide a comprehensive financial summary of the business. In reading these three financial statements did anything pique your curiosity? Did something in the financial statements stop you in your tracks and raise a question in your mind?

Well, one thing might have caught your attention. In its income statement for the year (Exhibit 2.2), the company reports that it earned $2,642,000 net income, or bottom-line profit. On the other hand, in its statement of cash flows for the year (Exhibit 2.3) the company reports that it generated $3,105,000 cash flow from operating activities, that is, from profit-making activities. In short, profit is $2,642,00 and cash flow from profit is $3,105,000 for the year.

Wait a minute: How can cash flow from profit be higher than profit? Where did the "extra" cash come from? In other situations could cash flow be less than profit? A simple answer is that profit, or more accurately the revenue and expenses that determine profit consist of more than just cash flows. Actual cash inflow from revenue is typically higher or lower that the amount of revenue recorded for the period. And, actual cash outflows for expenses are typically higher or lower than the amounts of expenses recorded for the period.

The first section of the statement of cash flows (see Exhibit 2.3 for instance) attempts to explain the differences between cash flows and revenue and expenses. But in our experience business managers, lenders, and investors generally cannot make heads or tails of this section of the cash flows statement. The main reason is that they don't have a clear picture of how revenue and expenses are recorded. Do you?

In this chapter we explain profit accounting fundamentals. We focus on the assets and liabilities used in recording revenue and expenses. The increases or decreases in these assets and liabilities during the period tell the tale of why cash flows differ from revenue and expenses. Directing attention to these changes opens the door to understanding cash flow from profit-making (operating) activities.

Having read this chapter you'll have a leg up in understanding what the first section of the statement of cash flows is trying to tell you.

Nature of Profit

Profit does not appear magically in the accounts of a business. The amount of profit for a period arises from recording revenue and expenses during the period. Recording revenue and expenses follow basic rules:

	Asset	Liability
Revenue	+	−
Expenses	−	+

Put into words, revenue increases an asset or decreases a liability. Expenses decrease an asset or increase a liability.

Revenue minus expenses equals profit. We're sure you have heard this many times. What you may not have heard is that profit equals the change in assets from revenue and expenses minus the change in liabilities from revenue and expenses. For example, consider the following scenario:

	Assets	Liabilities
Revenue	+$ 65	$ 0
Expenses	−$ 40	+$15
Net Change	+$ 25	+$15

What's profit for the period in this scenario? Assets increased $25 and liabilities increased $15—so profit equals $10. Notice that profit consists of a mix of changes in assets and liabilities. This point is extremely important to understand. Profit is not a single asset thing. Profit involves several assets, and liabilities as well.

Employing several different assets and liabilities to record revenue and expenses complicates profit accounting. But this method produces the truest measure of profit for the period. It's called *accrual basis* accounting. To be frank *accrual* is not a good descriptor for this profit accounting method. The term basically means that revenue and expenses are recorded when things happen—that is, when sales take place and when expenses are incurred. It might be better to call accrual basis accounting *real time* accounting.

What's the alternative? Well, revenue and expenses could be recorded when cash is received from sales and when expenses are paid. This method is called *cash basis* accounting. Cash basis accounting would be woefully inadequate and seriously misleading for most businesses, large or small, new or old, public or private. At this point refer to Exhibit 3.1. On the left this exhibit starts with the single-step income statement for the example we introduce in Chapter 2. On the right side the exhibit lists the balance sheet changes during the year for the asset and liabilities that are connected with revenue and expenses. Such a listing of balance sheet changes is not

EXHIBIT 3.1—INCOME STATEMENT AND BALANCE SHEET CHANGES DURING YEAR FROM PROFIT-MAKING ACTIVITIES

Dollar Amounts in Thousands

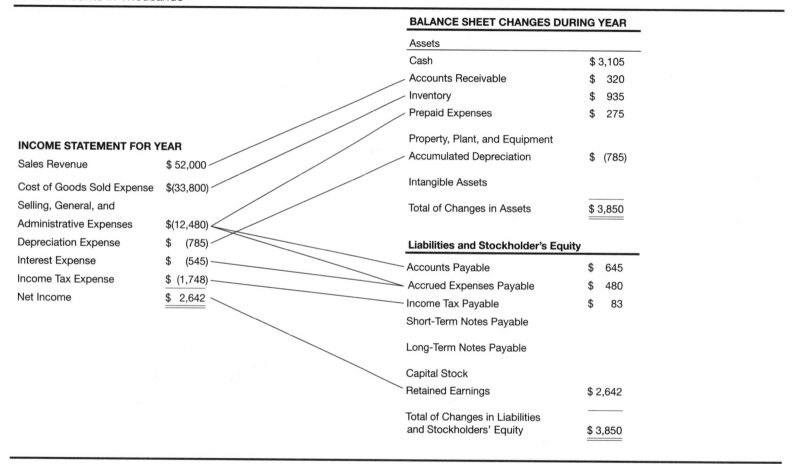

BALANCE SHEET CHANGES DURING YEAR

Assets

Cash	$ 3,105
Accounts Receivable	$ 320
Inventory	$ 935
Prepaid Expenses	$ 275
Property, Plant, and Equipment	
Accumulated Depreciation	$ (785)
Intangible Assets	
Total of Changes in Assets	$ 3,850

INCOME STATEMENT FOR YEAR

Sales Revenue	$ 52,000
Cost of Goods Sold Expense	$(33,800)
Selling, General, and Administrative Expenses	$(12,480)
Depreciation Expense	$ (785)
Interest Expense	$ (545)
Income Tax Expense	$ (1,748)
Net Income	$ 2,642

Liabilities and Stockholder's Equity

Accounts Payable	$ 645
Accrued Expenses Payable	$ 480
Income Tax Payable	$ 83
Short-Term Notes Payable	
Long-Term Notes Payable	
Capital Stock	
Retained Earnings	$ 2,642
Total of Changes in Liabilities and Stockholders' Equity	$ 3,850

regularly prepared (although a business manager could ask the accountant for such a report).

Lines of connection are shown between revenue and expenses in the income statement and the particular assets and liabilities in the balance sheet that are used in recording revenue and expenses. Notice that there are blanks in the changes column for several balance sheet items. Recording revenue and expenses do not affect these assets, liabilities, and the capital stock account.

There are no lines of connection to or from the cash account. We would have to draw too many lines because cash is extensively connected with most other balance sheet accounts.

Recording Revenue and Expenses

In the following sections we emphasize the particular assets and liabilities accountants use for recording revenue and expenses in accrual basis accounting. Our purpose is to make you mindful that the sales and expense activities of a business increase or decrease various assets and liabilities. The balance sheet of a business is driven in large part by its sales and expense transactions. Please refer to Exhibit 3.1 as we consider each line in the income statement.

Recording Revenue

In our company example the business makes all sales on credit. It offers its customers 30 days before they have to pay the business for their purchases. The business records sales on credit immediately on closing the sale and delivering the products to the customer. The business records this entry:

Income Statement:	**+ Sales Revenue**
Balance Sheet:	**+ Accounts Receivable**

See the line of connection in Exhibit 3.1 between Sales Revenue in the income statement and the *Accounts Receivable* asset in the balance sheet.

Over the year the business makes credit sales totaling $52,000,000. Therefore, $52,000,000 of increases was recorded in its Accounts Receivable asset account. As cash is collected from customers the cash account is increased, and Accounts Receivable is decreased the same amount.

Side note: A business may receive cash from customers before goods or services are delivered to them. One example is newspapers that collect subscriptions before the papers are delivered. When cash is received a liability account called *unearned revenue* (or equivalent title) is increased. As the business delivers the product or service it decreases the liability account and increases the revenue account. The business in our example does not collect money from customers in advance of delivery products to them.

During the year the business collected slightly less cash from customers than its sales revenue for the year. As a result the balance in Accounts Receivable increased $320,000 (see Exhibit 3.1). Chapter 5 explains further the cash flow from making credit sales and collecting accounts receivable.

Recording Cost of Goods Sold Expense

The business in our example sells products. The business needs to have products ready for sale and immediate delivery to its customers. So the business stockpiles a sizable collection of products. The company manufactures some of the products it sells and it buys other products that it resells to its customers. When it manufactures and buys products the cost amount of the acquisition is recorded as an increase in the *inventory* asset account. The cost of the products remains in the inventory asset account until the products are sold.

When products are sold their cost is removed from the inventory asset account and charged to Cost of Goods Sold Expense. The business makes this entry:

Income Statement: **+ Cost of Goods Sold Expense**
Balance Sheet: **– Inventory**

See the line of connection in Exhibit 3.1 between Cost of Goods Sold Expense in the income statement and the Inventory asset in the balance sheet. Total Cost of Goods Sold Expense for the year is $33,800,000, and the inventory asset account was decreased this amount during the year. The business made purchases during the year to replenish its stock of products as sales were made during the year.

The cash outflow for manufacturing and buying inventory during the year depends on whether the business decides to increase or decrease its level of inventory during the year—as well as other factors. During the year the business bought more inventory than it sold. Therefore, inventory increased $935,000 (see Exhibit 3.1). This increase in inventory required additional cash outlay during the year. We discuss further the company's ending inventory level and cash outflow for inventory purchases in Chapter 6.

Recording Selling, General, and Administrative (SG&A) Expenses

Like all businesses the company in our example has many kinds of operating expenses, which are lumped under the broad category of *Selling, General, and Administrative (SG&A) Expenses*. See Exhibit 3.1. This includes everything from the compensation of the president of the business to the cost of electricity. A good chunk is spent on advertising and marketing the products sold by the business. However, this group of expenses does not include the expenses for depreciation, interest, and income tax, which are reported separately in its income statement (see Exhibit 3.1).

Some selling, general, and administrative expenses are recorded by decreasing the cash asset account—no other asset or liability account is involved. Some are recorded by decreasing the prepaid expenses asset account. Some are recorded by increasing the accounts payable liability account. And, some are recorded by increasing the accrued expenses payable liability account.

Recording expenses when cash payments are made is straightforward:

Income Statement: **+ SG&A Expenses**
Balance Sheet: **– Cash**

Note: Recording an expense when cash payment is made assumes that the amount of expense is the correct amount to charge against revenue in the period.

The business has to prepay certain operating expenses, for example, insurance premiums. These prepayments benefit several future months. When the business makes a prepayment it initially records the amount in the *prepaid expenses* asset account. Then, the amounts of prepayments are allocated over the months benefited by the prepayment.

The prepayments are moved to expense by the following entry:

Income Statement: **+ SG&A Expenses**
Balance Sheet: **– Prepaid Expenses**

During the year the business prepaid for more of such expenses than it charged to selling, general, and administration expenses to the year. Thus, its prepaid expenses asset account increased $275,000 during the year (see Exhibit 3.1). We explain further the cash flow of prepaying expenses in Chapter 9.

The company in our example has been in business several years and has established a good credit rating. Therefore, the vendors and suppliers it makes purchases from extend the business normal credit terms. Also, the company uses business credit cards for travel and entertainment by its salespersons and officers.

When the business buys something on credit and uses its credit cards for purchases that should be charged to expense, the business records these short-term payables in the *Accounts Payable* liability account and makes the following entry:

Income Statement: **+ SG&A Expenses**
Balance Sheet: **+ Accounts Payable**

During the year the company ran up the amount of payables from purchases on credit and using credit cards. It paid out less than the total that was recorded in its accounts payable liability account. So this liability account increased $645,000 (see Exhibit 3.1). We explain further the cash flow of buying on credit in Chapter 8.

Some operating expenses accumulate over time. The business does not get an invoice for these costs. It has to recognize the gradual buildup of these costs. For example, the business provides vacation and sick pay for its employees. After 50 weeks an employee is entitled to take two weeks paid vacation. To record such expenses as they accumulate over time, a business uses a liability account called *Accrued Expenses Payable* (or equivalent title) and makes the following entry:

Income Statement: **+ SG&A Expenses**
Balance Sheet: **– Accrued Expenses Payable**

During the year the company paid less cash than the charges to its accrued expenses payable liability. So this liability increased $480,000 (see Exhibit 3.1). We explain further the cash flow of this liability account in Chapter 11.

Recording Depreciation Expense

The business in our example needs a warehouse to house the products it sells. And, it needs shelving, forklifts, and other equipment for handling and transporting the products. Also the business needs office space, as well as computers and office equipment and furniture. The business has invested $16,500,000 in various long-term operating assets, which are labeled *Property, Plant, and Equipment* in the balance sheet (see Exhibit 2.1).

The costs of these *fixed assets* (as they are also called) are not charged to expense immediately upon acquisition. Since fixed assets have useful lives of more than one year the cost of a fixed asset (except land) is charged piecemeal to expense over its estimated useful life to the business. Each year of using a fixed asset bears a share of the cost. The portion of cost allocated to a year is called *depreciation*. As you see in Exhibit 3.1 the business recorded $785,000 *Depreciation Expense* in the year.

Depreciation is recorded as follows:

Income Statement: **+ Depreciation Expense**
Balance Sheet: **– Accumulated Depreciation**

The accumulated depreciation account is an offset, or deduction against the cost of the fixed assets. It can be thought of as the negative side of the fixed assets account. In the balance sheet (refer to Exhibit 2.1, for instance) the balance in accumulated depreciation is deducted from the cost of property, plant, and equipment. An increase in this offset, or contra account has the effect of reducing the balance of property, plant, and equipment. In short, fixed assets are decreased $785,000 by recording depreciation.

Recording depreciation expense does not involve cash payment in the period the expense is recorded. Cash was paid when the fixed assets were purchased or constructed. We explain further the nature of depreciation expense and the central role of depreciation in analyzing cash flow in Chapter 10.

Recording Interest Expense

The business has borrowed sizable amounts on short-term and long-term notes payable (refer back to its balance sheet in Exhibit 2.1). The business has to pay interest for the use of this money. Interest accrues day by day. Interest is paid quarterly or semi-annually, or even just once a year. To recognize the accumulation of interest the business makes the following entry:

Income Statement: **+ Interest Expense**
Balance Sheet: **+ Accrued Expenses Payable**

When interest is paid the business decreases the liability account and decreases the cash account. We explain further the cash flow differences between recording interest and paying interest in Chapter 11.

Recording Income Tax Expense

For the year just ended the business has taxable income that resulted in Income Tax Expense of $1,748,000 (see Exhibit 3.1). To record this expense the business makes the following entry:

Income Statement: **+ Income Tax Expense**
Balance Sheet: **+ Income Tax Payable**

During the year a business is generally required to make installment payments on its estimated federal income tax for the year.

In fact, most of the income tax for the year should be paid over to the IRS by the end of the year. When the business makes installment payments to the IRS it decreases cash and decreases income tax payable. We explain further the cash flow effects of income tax expense and its liability in Chapter 12.

Recording Net Income into Retained Earnings

The net income for the year, as you undoubtedly know, equals sales revenue for the year minus the sum of expenses for the year. This bottom line net income amount is entered in the retained earnings owners' equity account. We won't bother you with the bookkeeping steps here, but the final effect is to increase retained earnings $2,642,000, which is the net income for the year (see Exhibit 3.1). The retained earnings stockholders' equity account in the balance sheet is the final home of profit.

The total of changes in the assets used to record revenue and expenses minus the total of changes in the liabilities used to measure revenue and expenses produces a net gain of $2,642,000 in the owners' equity. The *net worth* of the business, that is, its assets minus its liabilities, increases $2,642,000 from making profit—and this increase belongs to the owners. Their equity in the business is this much better off from earning profit.

Once the $2,642,000 net income amount is entered in retained earnings the balance sheet is in balance. The amount of total assets on the one side equals the amount of liabilities plus owners' equity on the other side. In our example the company's assets increased $3,850,000 during the year from its profit-making activities (see Exhibit 3.1). Deducting the $1,208,000 increase in liabilities from its operating activities gives a net increase of $2,642,000, which is profit (net income) for the year.

Winding Up

The business example presented in Exhibit 3.1 illustrates that making profit results in changes in several different assets and liabilities—not just cash. Cash is at the center of it, but several other assets are changed by a company's profit-making operations and so are certain liabilities. Business managers, creditors, and investors should understand and keep an eye on these changes. We stress this point repeatedly throughout the book.

Finally, let's circle back to the question that kick-started this chapter. Why did cash increase $3,105,000 during the period even though net income is only $2,642,000 for the period (see Exhibit 3.1)? In other words, why is cash flow $463,000 higher than profit for the period? There are several reasons.

In Exhibit 3.1 look again at the changes in assets and liabilities. Take the $320,000 increase in accounts receivable, for instance. This asset increase tells us that $320,000 less cash was collected from customers than sales revenue during the period. In general an increase in an asset has an unfavorable impact on cash flow, and a decrease has a favorable impact.

The cash flow impacts of changes in liabilities are the reverse of changes in assets. The $645,000 increase in accounts payable, for instance, tells us that $645,000 less cash was paid out during the year than the amount of expenses recorded in this liability. In general an increase in a liability has a favorable impact on cash flow, and a decrease has an unfavorable impact.

The cash flow effects of the changes in assets and liabilities are summarized as follows:

Cash Flow Impacts of Changes in Assets and Liabilities during the Year (from Exhibit 3.1)

Accounts Receivable increase	$(320,000)
Inventory increase	$(935,000)
Prepaid Expenses increase	$(275,000)
Accumulated Depreciation decrease	$ 785,000
Accounts Payable increase	$ 645,000
Accrued Expenses Payable increase	$ 480,000
Income Tax Payable increase	$ 83,000
Net effect on cash flow	$463,000

Recall that accumulated depreciation is a negative, or offset amount that is deducted from the cost of fixed assets. The increase in this account is in essence a decrease in the fixed assets being depreciated. Also, keep in mind that recording depreciation expense does not require a cash outlay. Thus, depreciation has a favorable impact on cash flow (more on this in Chapter 10).

The above summary shows the reasons why cash flow is $463,000 higher than profit for the period. If one of the changes had been different then cash flow would have been different. Suppose, for example, that accounts payable had not changed during the year. Cash flow from profit would have been $645,000 smaller, and in fact it would have been lower than profit for the year.

4

PROFIT ISN'T EVERYTHING

Threefold Financial Task of Business Managers

In Chapter 2 we introduce the three primary financial statements for a representative business example—the income statement, the balance sheet, and the statement of cash flows. We start this chapter by calling your attention to stockholders' equity in the balance sheet. Its owners have invested $8,125,000 capital in the business for which it issued capital stock shares to them. See the *capital stock* account in Exhibit 2.1. Furthermore, over the years the business has retained $15,000,000 profit, which is called *retained earnings*. Taken together these two sources of owners' equity equal $23,125,000. One purpose of the balance sheet is to disclose such information about the ownership of the business entity and the sources of its equity capital.

The stockholders expect the managers of the business to earn a reasonable annual profit on their $23,125,000 equity in the business. In its most recent annual income statement the business reports $2,642,000 bottom-line profit, or net income. Profit equals 11 percent on the company's year-end stockholders' equity. The stockholders, as well as the company's managers and its lenders, want to know more than just bottom-line profit. They want to see the whole picture of how profit is earned. Therefore, the income statement reports totals for revenue and expenses for the period as well as bottom-line net income.

The ability of managers to make sales and to control expenses, and thereby earn profit, is summarized in the income statement. Business investors and lenders pay particular attention to the profit yield from revenue. Earning profit is essential for survival and the business manager's most important financial imperative. But the bottom line is not the end of the manager's job, not by a long shot!

To earn profit and stay out of trouble, managers must control the *financial condition* of the business. This means, among other things, keeping assets and liabilities within appropriate limits and proportions relative to each other and relative to the sales revenue and expenses of the business. Managers must prevent cash shortages that would cause the business to default on its liabilities when they come due, or not be able to meet its payroll on time.

Business managers really have a threefold financial task: earning enough profit, controlling the company's assets and liabilities, and generating cash flows. For all businesses, regardless of size, a financial statement is prepared for each financial imperative—one for profit performance (the income statement), one for financial condition (the balance sheet), and the statement of cash flows.

Earning adequate profit by itself does not guarantee survival and good cash flow. A business manager cannot fully manage profit without also managing the assets and liabilities of sales revenue and expenses. We identify these assets and liabilities in Chapter 3 where we explain accrual basis profit accounting. In our business example, the changes in these assets and liabilities cause cash flow to be higher than the profit for the year. In other situations the changes can cause cash flow from profit to be less, perhaps much less, than profit for the period (and can cause negative cash flow in extreme situations).

Business managers use their income statements to evaluate profit performance and to ask a raft of profit-oriented questions. Did sales revenue meet the goals and objectives for the period? Why did sales revenue increase compared with last period? Which expenses increased more or less than they should have? And there are many more such questions. These profit analysis questions are absolutely essential. But the manager can't stop at the end of these questions.

Beyond profit analysis, business managers should move on to financial condition analysis and cash flows analysis. In large business corporations, the responsibility for financial condition and cash flow is separated from profit responsibility. The chief financial officer (CFO) of the company is responsible for financial condition and cash flow. The chief executive and board of directors oversee the CFO. They need to see the big picture, which includes all three financial aspects of the business—profit, financial condition, and cash flow.

In smaller businesses, however, the president or the owner/manager is directly involved in controlling financial condition and cash flow. There's no one to whom to delegate these responsibilities—although, consultants and advisors can be hired for advice.

One Problem in Reporting Financial Statements

Chapter 2 introduces the balance sheet, income statement, and statement of cash flows for a business example, as you would see these three primary financial statements in a typical financial report. Each of the statements stands alone, by itself, usually on a separate page in the financial report. Each statement is presented like a tub standing on its own feet. The "water pipes" (interconnections) between the three financial statements are not made explicit. There is no clear trail of the crossover effects between the three financial statements.

Unfortunately, the way financial statements are presented in a financial report does not make clear that making profit drives the financial condition and cash flows of the business. You can easily miss the vital interplay among the income statement, balance sheet, and statement of cash flows. Accountants assume that readers understand the couplings and linkages between the three financial statements and make use of these connections in analyzing the financial affairs of a business.

Chapter 3 provides a good start for understanding the connections between the income statement and the balance sheet. In Chapter 3 we identify the assets and liabilities used in recording revenue and expenses. The connections between revenue and expenses and their corresponding assets and liabilities are shown in Exhibit 3.1 (which you might want to take a quick look at again). The exhibit, however, does not show the other connections between the financial statements.

Exhibit 4.1 presents a comprehensive overview of the connections between the income statement and the balance sheet, and the connections between the changes in the balance sheet accounts and the statement of cash flows. The three financial statements fit together like tongue-in-groove woodwork; the income statement, balance sheet, and cash flows statement interlock with one another.

EXHIBIT 4.1—CONNECTIONS BETWEEN THE THREE FINANCIAL STATEMENTS
Dollar Amounts in Thousands

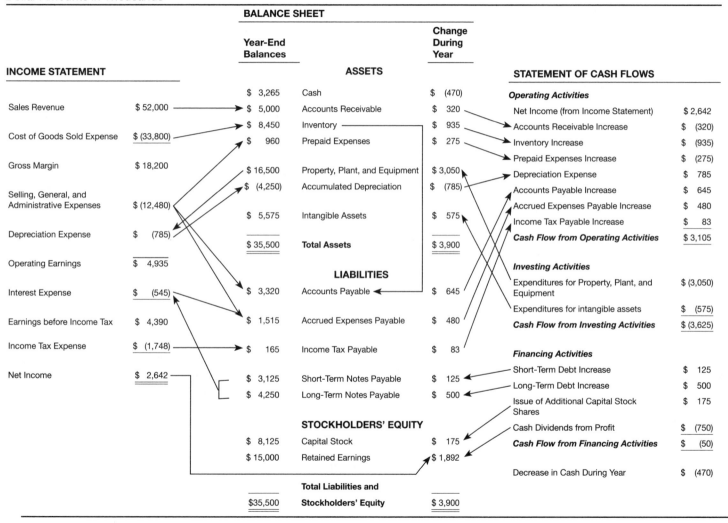

BALANCE SHEET

	Year-End Balances		Change During Year

INCOME STATEMENT

Sales Revenue	$ 52,000
Cost of Goods Sold Expense	$ (33,800)
Gross Margin	$ 18,200
Selling, General, and Administrative Expenses	$ (12,480)
Depreciation Expense	$ (785)
Operating Earnings	$ 4,935
Interest Expense	$ (545)
Earnings before Income Tax	$ 4,390
Income Tax Expense	$ (1,748)
Net Income	$ 2,642

ASSETS

Year-End Balances		Change During Year
$ 3,265	Cash	$ (470)
$ 5,000	Accounts Receivable	$ 320
$ 8,450	Inventory	$ 935
$ 960	Prepaid Expenses	$ 275
$ 16,500	Property, Plant, and Equipment	$ 3,050
$ (4,250)	Accumulated Depreciation	$ (785)
$ 5,575	Intangible Assets	$ 575
$ 35,500	**Total Assets**	$ 3,900

LIABILITIES

$ 3,320	Accounts Payable	$ 645
$ 1,515	Accrued Expenses Payable	$ 480
$ 165	Income Tax Payable	$ 83
$ 3,125	Short-Term Notes Payable	$ 125
$ 4,250	Long-Term Notes Payable	$ 500

STOCKHOLDERS' EQUITY

$ 8,125	Capital Stock	$ 175
$ 15,000	Retained Earnings	$ 1,892
$35,500	**Total Liabilities and Stockholders' Equity**	$ 3,900

STATEMENT OF CASH FLOWS

Operating Activities	
Net Income (from Income Statement)	$ 2,642
Accounts Receivable Increase	$ (320)
Inventory Increase	$ (935)
Prepaid Expenses Increase	$ (275)
Depreciation Expense	$ 785
Accounts Payable Increase	$ 645
Accrued Expenses Payable Increase	$ 480
Income Tax Payable Increase	$ 83
Cash Flow from Operating Activities	$ 3,105
Investing Activities	
Expenditures for Property, Plant, and Equipment	$ (3,050)
Expenditures for intangible assets	$ (575)
Cash Flow from Investing Activities	$ (3,625)
Financing Activities	
Short-Term Debt Increase	$ 125
Long-Term Debt Increase	$ 500
Issue of Additional Capital Stock Shares	$ 175
Cash Dividends from Profit	$ (750)
Cash Flow from Financing Activities	$ (50)
Decrease in Cash During Year	$ (470)

Interlocking Nature of the Three Financial Statements

Note: In Exhibit 4.1 the balance sheet is presented in the *vertical*, or portrait format, also called the *report form*—assets on top, and liabilities and stockholders' equity below. To save space we do not include subtotals for current assets, current liabilities, and stockholders' equity in the balance sheet. (You might quickly compare the balance sheet in Exhibit 4.1 with the "official" balance sheet example in Exhibit 2.1.)

In Chapter 3 we explain the connections between revenue and expenses in the income statement and their assets and liabilities in the balance sheet (see Exhibit 3.1). These connections are shown again in Exhibit 4.1—except that the lines of connection are to the *ending balances* of the assets and liabilities. In the following chapters we examine how large these ending balances in assets and liabilities should be relative to the amounts of revenue and expenses for the year.

In addition to ending balances Exhibit 4.1 shows the *changes* in the balance sheet accounts during the year. These changes go to or come from the statement of cash flows. The first section of the statement uses the changes in the assets and liabilities of recording revenue and expenses to reconcile net income and *cash flow from operating activities*. This important cash flow number is the net increase or decrease in cash that is attributable to the profit-making (operating) activities of the business.

The cash increase from the company's profit-making activities for the year is $3,105,000 (see Exhibit 4.1), which compared with its $2,642,000 net income is a fairly significant difference.

In this particular example, the company's cash flow from profit is $463,000 higher than its profit for the year. In Chapter 3 we explain how to use the changes in assets and liabilities of recording revenue and expenses to determine the difference between cash flow and profit.

The other, or nonoperating cash flows of the business during the year are reported in the *investing* and *financing* sections of the statement of cash flows. See Exhibit 4.1 again. The business made key decisions during the year that required major outlays of cash and secured additional cash during the year from its lenders and stockholders. Notice that the lines of connection for these cash flow decisions go from the cash flow sources and uses to their respective assets, liabilities, and stockholders' equity.

You really can't swallow all the information in Exhibit 4.1 in one gulp. You have to drink one sip at a time. Exhibit 4.1 serves as the road map that we refer to frequently in the following chapters—so that we don't lose sight of the big picture as we travel down the particular highways of connection between the financial statements.

Before moving on, we should stress that financial statements are not presented with lines of connection as shown in Exhibit 4.1. You never see tether lines like this between the financial statements. Accountants assume that the financial statement readers mentally fill in the connections that are shown in Exhibit 4.1. Accountants assume too much, in our opinion. It would be helpful if a financial report included reminders of the connections among the three financial statements. But don't hold your breath.

Connecting the Dots

In our experience, business managers and executives, and for that matter even some certified public accountants (CPAs) do not recognize the connecting links among the financial statements that we show in Exhibit 4.1. Over the years the senior author (John) has corresponded with many persons via email who requested the Microsoft Excel workbook file of the exhibits in this book. (See the Preface for John's e-mail address.) Over and over they mention one point—the value of seeing the connections among the financial statements.

John did not fully understand these connections himself until he started teaching at the University of California at Berkeley in 1961. In browsing through an old, out-of-print textbook, he came upon the point that financial statements, although presented separately, are articulated with one another. Even though John had already had earned his PhD, he had not seen this critical point before. (Perhaps he had slept through that particular lecture.) He was struck by the term *articulated*. In his mind's eye John could see an articulated bus, a bus having two compartments that were connected together.

Exhibit 4.1 provides the framework for the following chapters. We think you will find the financial trips in the following chapters interesting and helpful.

Part Two

CONNECTIONS

5

SALES REVENUE AND ACCOUNTS RECEIVABLE

EXHIBIT 5.1—SALES REVENUE AND ACCOUNTS RECEIVABLE
Dollar Amounts in Thousands

BALANCE SHEET AT YEAR-END

ASSETS

Cash	$ 3,265
Accounts Receivable	$ 5,000
Inventory	$ 8,450
Prepaid Expenses	$ 960
Property, Plant, and Equipment	$ 16,500
Accumulated Depreciation	$ (4,250)
Intangible Assets	$ 5,575
Total Assets	$ 35,500

LIABILITIES AND STOCKHOLDERS' EQUITY

Accounts Payable	$ 3,320
Accrued Expenses Payable	$ 1,515
Income Tax Payable	$ 165
Short-Term Notes Payable	$ 3,125
Long-Term Notes Payable	$ 4,250
Capital Stock	$ 8,125
Retained Earnings	$15,000
Total Liabilities and Stockholders' Equity	$ 35,500

INCOME STATEMENT FOR YEAR

Sales Revenue	$ 52,000
Cost of Goods Sold Expense	$ (33,800)
Selling, General, and Administrative Expenses	$ (12,480)
Depreciation Expense	$ (785)
Interest Expense	$ (545)
Income Tax Expense	$ (1,748)
Net Income	$ 2,642

Assuming five weeks of annual sales revenue is uncollected at year-end the ending balance of Accounts Receivable is:

$5/52 \times \$52,000 = \$5,000$

Exploring One Link at a Time

Please refer to Exhibit 5.1 at the start of the chapter, which shows the connection between *sales revenue* in the income statement and the *accounts receivable* asset account in the balance sheet. This exhibit is taken from Exhibit 4.1 in Chapter 4. Exhibit 4.1 presents the big picture; it ties together all the connections between the three financial statements. This chapter is the first of many that focus on just one connection at a time. Only one line of connection is highlighted in Exhibit 5.1—the one between sales revenue in the income statement and accounts receivable in the balance sheet.

Friendly reminder: In Exhibit 5.1 (and all the exhibits in the coming chapters) the income statement and balance sheet are stripped of subtotals. For example, the income statement is a single-step statement, meaning that no lines are shown for gross margin and other intermediate measures of profit. Likewise, in the balance sheet no subtotals are shown for current assets and current liabilities and for the amount of property, plant, and equipment less accumulated depreciation.

Excluding subtotals gives us lean and mean financial statements to work with.

Another friendly reminder: Exhibit 5.1 does not include the company's statement of cash flows for the year. The connections between changes in the balance sheet accounts and the cash flows statement are explained in Chapters 14 and 15. The cash flows statement would be a distraction at this point.

The central idea in this and following chapters is that the profit-making activities reported in the income statement drive or determine an asset or a liability. Assets and liabilities are reported in the balance sheet. In our example the company's sales revenue for the year just ended was $52 million. Of this total sales revenue, $5 million is in the accounts receivable asset account at the end of the year. The $5 million is that part of annual sales that has not yet been collected at the end of the year.

In the following chapters we explore each linkage between an income statement account and its connecting account in the balance sheet.

How Sales Revenue Drives Accounts Receivable

In our business example, the company made $52,000,000 total sales during the year. This is a sizable amount, equal to $1,000,000 average sales revenue per week. When making a sale, the total amount of the sale (sales price times the quantity of products sold) is recorded in the *sales revenue* account. This account accumulates all sales made during the year. On the first day of the year it starts with a zero balance; at the end of the last day of the year it has a $52,000,000 balance. In short, the balance in this account at year-end is the sum of all sales for the entire year (assuming all sales are recorded).

In the example, the business makes all its sales on credit, which means that cash is not received until sometime after the time of sale. This company sells to other businesses that demand credit. (Many retailers, such as supermarkets and gas stations, make all sales for cash, or accept credit cards that are converted into cash immediately.) The amount owed to the company from making a sale on credit is immediately recorded in the accounts receivable asset account for the amount of each sale. (The entry for sales on credit is also explained in Chapter 3.) Sometime later, when cash is collected from customers, the cash account is increased and the accounts receivable account is decreased.

Extending credit to customers creates a cash inflow lag. The accounts receivable balance is the amount of this lag. At year-end the balance in this asset account is the amount of uncollected sales revenue. Most of the sales made on credit during the year have been converted into cash by the end of the year. Also, the accounts receivable balance at the start of the year from credit sales made last year was collected. But, many sales made during the latter part of the year just ended have not yet been collected by the end of the year. The total amount of these uncollected sales is found in the ending balance of accounts receivable.

Some of the company's customers pay quickly to take advantage of prompt payment discounts offered by the company. (These discounts off list prices reduce sales prices but speed up cash receipts.) However, the average customer waits five weeks to pay the company and forgoes the prompt payment discount. Some customers even wait 10 weeks or more to pay the company, despite the company's efforts to encourage them to pay sooner. The company puts up with these slow payers because they generate many repeat sales.

In sum, the company has a mix of quick, regular, and slow-paying customers. Suppose that the average credit period for all customers is five weeks. (This doesn't mean that every customer takes five weeks to pay, but rather that the average time before paying is five weeks.) Therefore, on average five weeks of annual sales are still uncollected at year-end. The relationship between annual sales revenue and the ending balance of accounts receivable can be expressed as follows:

$$\frac{5}{52} \times \frac{\$52,000,000 \text{ Sales}}{\text{Revenue for the Year}} = \frac{\$5,000,000 \text{ Accounts}}{\text{Receivable at End of Year}}$$

As you see in Exhibit 5.1, the ending balance of accounts receivable is $5,000,000; this amount equals five weeks of annual sales revenue. The main point is that the average sales credit period determines the size of accounts receivable. The longer the average sales credit period, the larger the accounts receivable amount.

Let's approach this key point from another direction. Suppose we didn't know the average credit period. Nevertheless, using information from the financial statements we can determine the average credit period. The first step is to calculate the following ratio:

$$\frac{\$52,000,000 \text{ Sales Revenue}}{\$5,000,000 \text{ Accounts Receivable}} = 10.4 \text{ Times}$$

This calculation gives the *accounts receivable turnover ratio*, which is 10.4 in this example. Dividing this ratio into 52 weeks gives the average sales credit period expressed in number of weeks:

$$\frac{52 \text{ Weeks}}{10.4 \text{ Accounts Receivable Turnover Ratio}} = 5 \text{ Weeks}$$

Time is the essence of the matter. What interests the business manager, and the company's creditors and investors as well, is how long it takes on average to turn accounts receivable into cash. We think the accounts receivable turnover ratio is most meaningful when it is used to determine the number of weeks (or days, if you like) it takes a company to convert its accounts receivable into cash.

You may argue that five weeks is too long an average sales credit period for the company. This is precisely the point: What should it be? The manager in charge has to decide whether the average credit period is getting out of hand. The manager can shorten credit terms, shut off credit to slow payers, or step up collection efforts.

This isn't the place to discuss customer credit policies relative to marketing strategies and customer relations, which would take us far beyond the field of accounting. But, to make an important point here, assume that without losing any sales the company's average sales credit period had been only four weeks, instead of five weeks.

In this alternative scenario, the company's ending accounts receivable balance would have been $1,000,000 less, or $4,000,000 (4/52 × $52,000,000 annual sales revenue = $4,000,000). The company would have collected $1,000,000 more cash during the year. With this additional cash, the company could have borrowed $1,000,000 less. At an annual 6 percent interest rate, this would have saved the business $60,000 interest before income tax. Or the owners could have invested $1,000,000 less in the business and put their money elsewhere.

The main point is that capital has a cost. Excess accounts receivable means that excess debt or excess owners' equity capital is being used by the business. The business is not as capital efficient as it should be.

A slowdown in collecting customers' receivables or a deliberate shift in business policy allowing longer credit terms causes accounts receivable to increase. Additional capital would have to be secured, or the company would have to attempt to get by on a smaller cash balance.

If you were the business manager in this example, you should decide whether the size of accounts receivable, being five weeks of annual sales revenue, is consistent with your company's sales credit terms and your collection policies. Perhaps five weeks is too long and you need to take action. If you were a creditor or an investor in the company, you should pay attention to whether the manager is allowing the average sales credit period to get out of control. A major change in the average credit period may signal a significant change in the company's policies.

Accounting Issues

Starting in this chapter and continuing in through Chapter 13 we focus on a key connection between an income statement account and its corresponding balance sheet account. We end these chapters with a brief discussion of some of the major accounting problems pertaining to the topics discussed in the chapter.

These short discussions of accounting issues barely scratch the surface. Nevertheless, you should be aware that the numbers you see in financial statements depend on the accounting methods used to recognize and record those numbers. The chief accounting officer of every business must decide which accounting methods to use to record sales revenue and expenses. These accounting decisions often require tough and somewhat arbitrary choices between alternative methods.

You may not be aware that accounting decisions are not entirely obvious and clear-cut in most situations. As a matter of fact, accounting methods are quite arbitrary to one degree or another in most cases. The choice of particular accounting methods makes profit lower or higher and also makes the amounts of assets and liabilities lower or higher. Remember the lesson about revenue and expenses from Chapter 3. Revenue is either an increase in an asset or a decrease in a liability. And, an expense is either a decrease in an asset or an increase in a liability.

So, what are the main issues in accounting for sales and accounts receivable? The main accounting problem in recording sales is *timing*. It's not always clear exactly when a sale is completed and all terms are final and definite. For instance, customers may have the right to return products they have purchased. Customers may have the right to take discounts from sales prices after the point of sale. Sales prices may still be negotiable even after the point of sale. Then, there are the costs of product warranties and guarantees to consider.

The asset generated by credit sales (i.e., accounts receivable) may end up being not collectible, or not fully collectible. When should the business record the expense for uncollectible receivables (called *bad debts*)?

In short, there are several serious problems surrounding accounting for sales. Therefore, a business should make clear in the footnotes to its financial statements the basic accounting method it uses for recording sales revenue.

6

COST OF GOODS SOLD EXPENSE AND INVENTORY

EXHIBIT 6.1—COST OF GOODS SOLD EXPENSE AND INVENTORY
Dollar Amounts in Thousands

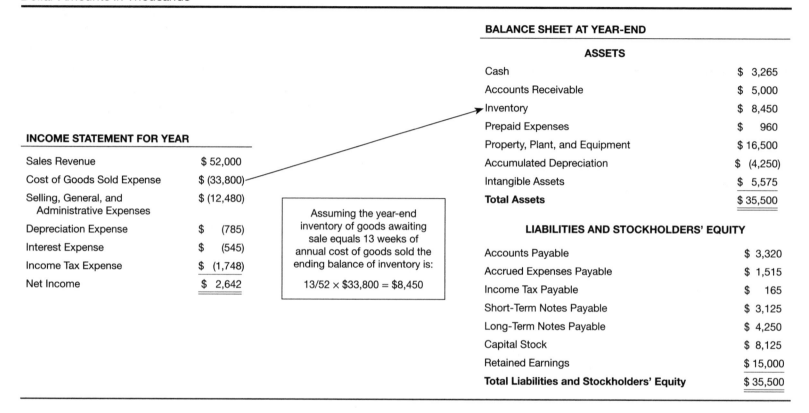

BALANCE SHEET AT YEAR-END

ASSETS

Cash	$ 3,265
Accounts Receivable	$ 5,000
Inventory	$ 8,450
Prepaid Expenses	$ 960
Property, Plant, and Equipment	$ 16,500
Accumulated Depreciation	$ (4,250)
Intangible Assets	$ 5,575
Total Assets	**$ 35,500**

LIABILITIES AND STOCKHOLDERS' EQUITY

Accounts Payable	$ 3,320
Accrued Expenses Payable	$ 1,515
Income Tax Payable	$ 165
Short-Term Notes Payable	$ 3,125
Long-Term Notes Payable	$ 4,250
Capital Stock	$ 8,125
Retained Earnings	$ 15,000
Total Liabilities and Stockholders' Equity	**$ 35,500**

INCOME STATEMENT FOR YEAR

Sales Revenue	$ 52,000
Cost of Goods Sold Expense	$ (33,800)
Selling, General, and Administrative Expenses	$ (12,480)
Depreciation Expense	$ (785)
Interest Expense	$ (545)
Income Tax Expense	$ (1,748)
Net Income	$ 2,642

> Assuming the year-end inventory of goods awaiting sale equals 13 weeks of annual cost of goods sold the ending balance of inventory is:
>
> 13/52 × $33,800 = $8,450

Please refer to Exhibit 6.1 at the start of the chapter. (Chapter 5 explains the design of this exhibit, which is also used in following chapters.) This chapter focuses on the connection between *cost of goods sold expense* in the income statement and the *inventory* asset in the balance sheet. Recall that the business in the example sells products, which are also called *goods* (in general) or *merchandise* (for retailers).

Holding Products in Inventory before They Are Sold

Cost of goods sold expense means just that—the cost of all products sold to customers during the year. The revenue from the sales is recorded in the sales revenue account, which is reported just above the cost of goods sold expense in the income statement (see Exhibit 6.1). Cost of goods sold expense is by far the largest expense in the company's income statement, being almost three times its selling, general, and administrative expenses for the year.

Putting cost of goods sold expense first, at the head of the expenses, is logical because it's the most direct and immediate cost of selling products. Please recall that this expense is deducted from sales revenue in income statements so that *gross margin* is reported there—see Exhibit 2.2 for an example of an income statement that reports gross margin. Although gross margin is not shown on a separate line in Exhibit 6.1, in order to focus on the key connections of income statement and balance sheet accounts, we can't emphasize enough the importance of gross margin (also called *gross profit*).

The word *gross* emphasizes that no other expenses have been deducted from sales revenue yet. There are more expenses that must be deducted before arriving at bottom-line profit (net income). Gross margin is the starting point for earning an adequate final, bottom-line profit for the period. In other words, the first step is to sell products for enough gross margin so that all other expenses can be covered and still leave an adequate remainder of profit. Later chapters discuss the company's other expenses.

You can do the arithmetic and determine that cost of goods sold expense equals 65 percent of sales revenue. Therefore, gross margin equals 35 percent of sales revenue. The business sells many different products, some for more than 35 percent gross margin and some for less. In total, for all products sold during the year, its average gross margin is 35 percent—which is fairly typical for a broad cross section of businesses. Gross margins more than 50 percent or less than 20 percent are unusual.

To sell products, most businesses must keep a stock of products on hand, which is called *inventory*. If a company sells products, it would be a real shock to see no inventory in its balance sheet (it is possible, but highly unlikely). Notice in Exhibit 6.1 that the line of connection is not between sales revenue and inventory, but between cost of goods sold expense and inventory. The inventory asset is reported at cost in the balance sheet, not at its sales value.

The inventory asset account accumulates the cost of the products purchased or manufactured. Acquisition cost stays in an inventory asset account until the products are sold to customers. At the time of sale, the cost of the products is removed from inventory and charged out to cost of goods sold expense. (Products may become nonsalable or may be stolen or damaged, in which case their cost is written down or removed from inventory and the amount is charged to cost of goods sold or some other expense, which we discuss at the end of the chapter.)

The company's inventory balance at year-end—$8,450,000 in the example—is the cost of products awaiting sale next year. The $33,800,000 deducted from sales revenue in the income statement is the cost of goods that were sold during the year. None of these products were on hand in year-end inventory.

Some of the company's products are manufactured in a short time, and some take much longer. Once the production process is finished, the products are moved into the company warehouse for storage until the goods are sold and delivered to customers. Some products are sold quickly, almost right off the end of the production line. Other products sit in the warehouse many weeks before being sold. Likewise, products bought from other companies may stay inventory only a short time or may remain in stock two or more months before being old. This business, like most companies, sells a mix of different products—some of which have very short holding periods and some relatively long holding periods.

In the example, the company's *average* inventory holding period for all products is 13 weeks, or three months on average. This time interval includes the production process time and the warehouse storage time. For example, a product may take three weeks to manufacture and then be held in storage 10 weeks, or vice versa. Internally, manufacturers separate "work-in-process" inventory (products still in the process of being manufactured) from "finished goods" (completed inventory ready for delivery to customers). For the products it buys from other companies in a condition ready for resell the business does not need a work-in-process account. Usually only one combined inventory account is reported in an external balance sheet, as shown in Exhibit 6.1. Internally, many separate inventory accounts are reported to managers.

Given that its average inventory holding period is 13 weeks, the company's inventory cost can be expressed as follows:

$$\frac{13}{52} \times \frac{\$33,800,000}{\text{Cost of Goods Sold Expense for Year}} = \begin{array}{c} \$8,450,000 \\ \text{Inventory} \\ \text{at End of Year} \end{array}$$

Notice in Exhibit 6.1 that the company's ending inventory balance is $8,450,000.

The main point is that the average inventory holding period determines the size of inventory relative to annual cost of goods sold expense. The longer the manufacturing and warehouse holding period, the larger is the inventory amount. Business managers prefer to operate with the lowest level of inventory possible, without causing lost sales due to products being out of stock when customers want to buy them. A business invests substantial capital in inventory.

Now, suppose we didn't know the company's average inventory holding period. Using information from its financial statements, we can determine the average inventory holding period.

The first step is to calculate the following ratio:

$$\frac{\$33,800,000 \text{ Cost of Goods Sold Expense}}{\$8,450,000 \text{ Inventory}} = 4.00 \text{ Times}$$

This gives the *inventory turnover ratio*. Dividing this ratio into 52 weeks gives the average inventory holding period expressed in number of weeks:

$$\frac{52 \text{ Weeks}}{4.00 \text{ Inventory Turnover Ratio}} = 13 \text{ Weeks}$$

$$\frac{10}{52} \times \begin{array}{c} \$33,800,000 \\ \text{Cost of Goods Sold} \\ \text{Expense for Year} \end{array} = \begin{array}{c} \$6,500,000 \\ \text{Ending Inventory} \end{array}$$

Time is the essence of the matter, as with the average sales credit period extended to customers. What interests the managers, as well as the company's creditors and investors, is how long the company holds inventory before products are sold. We think the inventory turnover ratio is most meaningful when used to determine the number of weeks (or days if you prefer) that it takes before inventory is sold.

Is 13 weeks too long? Should the company's average inventory holding period be shorter? These are precisely the key questions business managers, creditors, and investors should get answers to. If the holding period is longer than necessary, too much capital is being tied up in inventory. Or, the company may be cash poor because it keeps too much money in inventory and not enough in the bank.

To demonstrate this key point, suppose that with better inventory management the company could have reduced its average inventory holding period to, say, 10 weeks. This would have been a rather dramatic improvement. But modern inventory management techniques such as supply-chain management promise such improvement. If the company had reduced its average inventory holding period to just 10 weeks, its ending inventory would have been:

In this scenario ending inventory would be $1,950,000 smaller ($8,450,000 versus $6,500,000). The company would have needed $1,950,000 less capital, or would have had this much more cash balance at its disposal.

Caution: With only 10 weeks' inventory, the company may be unable to make some sales because certain products might not be available for immediate delivery to customers. In other words, if overall inventory is too low, stock-outs may occur. Nothing is more frustrating, especially to the sales staff, than having willing customers but no products to deliver to them. The cost of carrying inventory has to be balanced against the profit opportunities lost by not having products on hand ready for sale.

In summary, business managers, creditors, and investors should watch that the inventory holding period is neither too long nor too short. Call this the Goldilocks test. If too long, capital is being wasted; if too short, profit opportunities are being missed. Comparisons of a company's inventory holding period with those of its competitors and with historical trends provide useful benchmarks.

Accounting Issues

Accounting for cost of goods sold expense and the cost of inventory is beset with many problems. First of all, we should mention that businesses that manufacture the products have serious problems in determining the total cost per unit of the different products they produce. Believe us, this is no walk in the park.

College and university accounting programs offer one entire course on this topic (usually called cost accounting). One main problem is the allocation of *indirect* production costs to the different products that benefit from the cost. For example, how should you allocate the cost of security guards who patrol many production departments, or the depreciation on the production plant in which hundreds of different products are manufactured?

Retailers and wholesalers (distributors) buy products in a condition ready for resale. Compared with manufacturers, resellers have a much easier time determining the cost of the products they sell—although there are a few thorny problems. In any case, once acquisition costs have been recorded (for both manufacturers and resellers), another problem rears its ugly head: Product costs fluctuate over time. Period to period, product costs move up or down.

Suppose a business has acquired two units of a product, the first for $100 and the second for $104. The business sells one unit of the product. What is the correct cost to remove from the inventory asset account and to record in cost of goods sold expense? Accountants have come up with three different ways to answer this question: $100 (first-in, first-out); $102 (average cost); and, $104 (last-in, first-out). All three methods are acceptable. Different businesses use different methods.

You might think that a business would select the method that gives it the best match with its sales revenue, to get the best measure of gross margin. Generally speaking, the best method would be the one that is most consistent with how the business sets its sales prices. But this logic does not always prevail. A business selects a cost of goods sold method for other reasons, and the method may or may not jibe with its sales pricing policies.

The inventory asset account is written down to record losses from falling sales prices, lower replacement costs, damage and spoilage, and shrinkage (shoplifting and employee theft). The losses may be recorded in the cost of goods sold expense account, or be put in another expense account. Companies do not disclose where the losses from these write-downs are recorded.

Because a business has a choice of accounting methods, it should reveal its cost of goods sold expense method in the footnotes to its financial statements. If the business uses the last-in, first-out (LIFO) method, it should disclose in the footnote the approximate current cost value of its inventory as if it had been using the first-in, first-out (FIFO) method. Other unusual events, such as a major write-down of inventory, also should be disclosed in the footnote. Unfortunately, inventory footnotes are fairly technical and difficult to understand. We discuss footnotes to financial statements in Chapter 17.

7

INVENTORY AND ACCOUNTS PAYABLE

EXHIBIT 7.1—INVENTORY AND ACCOUNTS PAYABLE

Dollar Amounts in Thousands

BALANCE SHEET AT YEAR-END

ASSETS

Cash	$ 3,265
Accounts Receivable	$ 5,000
Inventory	$ 8,450
Prepaid Expenses	$ 960
Property, Plant, and Equipment	$ 16,500
Accumulated Depreciation	$ (4,250)
Intangible Assets	$ 5,575
Total Assets	$ 35,500

Assuming the amount payable at year-end for inventory related purchases is four weeks of the 13 weeks in inventory, the year-end balance of Accounts Payable for inventory is:

$$4/13 \times \$8,450 = \$2,600$$

INCOME STATEMENT FOR YEAR

Sales Revenue	$ 52,000
Cost of Goods Sold Expense	$ (33,800)
Selling, General, and Administrative Expenses	$ (12,480)
Depreciation Expense	$ (785)
Interest Expense	$ (545)
Income Tax Expense	$ (1,748)
Net Income	$ 2,642

LIABILITIES AND STOCKHOLDERS' EQUITY

Accounts Payable	$ 2,600	
Accounts Payable	$ 720	$ 3,320
Accrued Expenses Payable		$ 1,515
Income Tax Payable		$ 165
Short-Term Notes Payable		$ 3,125
Long-Term Notes Payable		$ 4,250
Capital Stock		$ 8,125
Retained Earnings		$ 15,000
Total Liabilities and Stockholders' Equity		$ 35,500

Acquiring Inventory on the Cuff

Please refer to Exhibit 7.1 at the start of the chapter. This chapter focuses on the connection between the *inventory* asset account in the balance sheet and the *accounts payable* liability in the balance sheet. Virtually every business reports accounts payable in its balance sheet, which is a short-term, noninterest-bearing liability arising from buying services, supplies, materials, and products on credit.

One main source of accounts payable is from making *inventory* purchases on credit. A second source of accounts payable is from *expenses* that are not paid immediately. Therefore, at this point we divide the total balance of the company's accounts payable liability into two parts, one for each source (refer to Exhibit 7.1 again).

The previous two chapters connect an income statement account with a balance sheet account. In this chapter we look at a connection between two balance sheet accounts. The linkage explained in this chapter is not about how sales revenue or an expense drives an asset, but rather how inventory drives its corresponding liability.

In our example the company purchases some products it sells and also manufactures other products. To begin the manufacturing process, the company purchases raw materials needed in its production process. These purchases are made on credit; the company doesn't pay for these purchases right away. Also, other production inputs are bought on credit. For example, once a month the public utility sends a bill for the gas and electricity used during the month, and the company takes several weeks before paying its utility bills. The company purchases several other manufacturing inputs on credit also. And, last but not least, the company sells products that it purchases from other manufacturers, and these are bought on credit. As you probably know, a business has to maintain its credit reputation and good standing to continue buying materials, manufacturing inputs, and products on credit.

Retailers and wholesalers (distributors) don't make the products they sell; they buy products and resell them. The products they buy are in a condition ready for resale. (Well, they may have to do some unpacking of large size containers, but you get the point.) Unless they have lousy credit ratings retailers and wholesalers buy on credit and they have accounts payable from inventory purchases. Technically speaking the company in our example is both a manufacturer of some products and a reseller of other products.

In the balance sheet shown in Exhibit 7.1, the company's $2,600,000 liability for inventory purchases on credit is presented as the first of two accounts payable amounts. The company's selling, general, and administrative expenses also generate accounts payable; the total amount of these unpaid bills ($720,000) is shown as the second accounts payable liability amount (see Exhibit 7.1 again). We discuss the second source of accounts payable in Chapter 8.

Typically, a company's inventory holding period is considerably longer than its purchase credit period. In other words, accounts payable are paid much quicker than it takes to sell inventory bought on credit. In this example, the company's average inventory holding period from the start of the production process or from the date of purchase to final sale of products averages 13 weeks (which we explain in Chapter 6). But the company has to pay its accounts payable in four weeks, on average.

Some purchases are paid for quickly, to take advantage of prompt payment discounts offered by vendors. The business takes six weeks or longer to pay many other invoices. Based on its experience and policies, a business knows the average purchase credit period for its inventory-related purchases. In this example, suppose the business takes four weeks on average to pay these liabilities.

Therefore, the year-end balance of accounts payable for inventory-related purchases on credit can be expressed as follows:

$$\frac{4}{13} \times \frac{\$8,450,000}{\text{Inventory}} = \frac{\$2,600,000}{\text{Accounts Payable}}$$

In short, this liability equals 4/13 of the inventory balance. The business gets a free ride for the first four weeks of holding inventory because it waits this long before paying for its purchases on credit. However, the remaining nine weeks of its inventory holding period have to be financed from debt and stockholders' equity sources of capital.

Economists are fond of saying that "there's no such thing as a free lunch." With this in mind, calling the four-week delay in paying for purchases on credit a free ride is not entirely accurate. Sellers that extend credit set their prices slightly higher to compensate for the delay in receiving cash from their customers. In other words, a small but hidden interest charge is built into the cost paid by the purchasers.

Accounting Issues

Several serious accounting issues concerning inventory are discussed at the end of Chapter 6. In sharp contrast, there are relatively few accounting problems as such concerning the accounts payable liability. The main financial reporting issue concerns *disclosure* of relevant information about this liability.

Financial statement readers are entitled to assume that the amount reported for accounts payable is the amount that will be paid in the near future. Suppose, however, that the business is in the middle of negotiations with one or more of its accounts payable creditors regarding prices and other terms. Suppose that these disagreements involve material (significant) amounts. In this situation, the business should make a disclosure about these negotiations in the footnotes to its financial statements.

Also, financial statement readers are entitled to assume that the company's accounts payable creditors (the parties to whom it owes money) do *not* have senior or prior claims ahead of other creditors and debtholders of the business. In other words, the accounts payable creditors are assumed to be *general* creditors of the business, with no special claims on the assets of the business. If in fact the accounts payable creditors have unusual rights for payment against the business, these abnormal claims should be disclosed in the footnotes to its financial statements.

Here is another important point: Financial statement readers are entitled to assume that the accounts payable are *current*, which means that the liabilities are not seriously overdue (i.e., way beyond their due dates for payment). Suppose, for instance, that half of the company's accounts payable are two or three months overdue. In this situation the business should disclose the overdue amount in the footnotes to its financial statements.

We may not need to emphasize this, but accounts payable are noninterest-bearing and should not be intermingled with the interest-bearing debts of the business. As you see in Exhibit 7.1, interest-bearing liabilities (notes payable) are reported in separate liability accounts. By the way, long-overdue accounts payable may begin to accrue interest at the option of the creditor.

We should mention that the disclosure standards we discuss here for accounts payable are not necessarily complied with in actual financial reports. You don't see much disclosure about accounts payable in business financial statements. We think a business should make full disclosure in its financial reports. But in fact companies are cut a lot of slack in the area of accounts payable. You don't find detailed information about a company's accounts payable liability in its financial statements, even though this particular liability may be more than 10 percent of a company's total assets and may be larger than its cash balance at the balance sheet date (as it is in our business example).

8

OPERATING EXPENSES AND ACCOUNTS PAYABLE

EXHIBIT 8.1—SELLING, GENERAL, AND ADMINISTRATIVE EXPENSES AND ACCOUNTS PAYABLE

Dollar Amounts in Thousands

Assuming three weeks of annual selling, general, and administrative expenses are unpaid at the end of the year, the year-end balance of accounts payable for these unpaid expenses is:

$$3/52 \times \$12,480 = \$720$$

INCOME STATEMENT FOR YEAR

Sales Revenue	$ 52,000
Cost of Goods Sold Expense	$ (33,800)
Administrative Expenses	$ (12,480)
Depreciation Expenses	$ (785)
Interest Expense	$ (545)
Income Tax Expenses	$ (1,748)
Net Income	$ 2,642

BALANCE SHEET AT YEAR-END

ASSETS

Cash		$ 3,265
Accounts Receivable		$ 5,000
Inventory		$ 8,450
Prepaid Expenses		$ 960
Property, Plant, and Equipment		$ 16,500
Accumulated Depreciation		$ (4,250)
Intangible Assets		$ 5,575
Total Assets		**$ 35,500**

LIABILITIES AND STOCKHOLDERS' EQUITY

Accounts Payable	$ 2,600	$ 3,320
Accrued Expenses Payable	$ 720	$ 1,515
Income Tax Payable		$ 165
Short-Term Notes Payable		$ 3,125
Long-Term Notes Payable		$ 4,250
Capital Stock		$ 8,125
Retained Earnings		$ 15,000
Total Liabilities and Stockholders' Equity		**$ 35,500**

Recording Expenses before They Are Paid

Please refer to Exhibit 8.1 at the start of the chapter, which highlights the connection between *selling, general, and administrative expenses* in the income statement and the second of the two *accounts payable* components in the balance sheet. Recall from Chapter 7 the two sources of accounts payable—from inventory purchases on credit, and from expenses not paid immediately. Chapter 7 explains the connection between inventory and accounts payable. This chapter explains how expenses drive the accounts payable liability of a business.

Every business in the world has a wide variety of operating expenses. The term *operating* does *not* include cost of goods sold, interest, and income tax expenses. Also, in our example, the company's depreciation expense is reported separately. All other operating expenses are combined into one conglomerate account labeled "Selling, General, and Administrative Expenses" (see the income statement in Exhibit 8.1). This expense title is widely used by businesses, although you see variations.

Day in and day out, many operating expenses are recorded when they are paid, at which time an expense account is increased and the cash account is decreased. (Chapter 3 explains the recording of these types of expenses.) But some operating expenses have to be recorded *before* they are paid—which is the focus of this chapter.

Operating expenses is the convenient term that we use in the collective sense to refer to many different specific expenses of running

(operating) a business enterprise. In this business example, the annual depreciation expense on the company's long-lived, fixed assets is shown as a separate expense. So, the $12,480,000 total amount of selling, general, and administrative expenses does not include depreciation. (It would if the depreciation expense were not reported separately.) And, to remind you, the $12,480,000 total for operating expenses does not include cost of goods sold, interest, and income tax expenses, which are reported separately in the income statement (see Exhibit 8.1 again).

Operating expenses include the following specific expenses (in no particular order):

♦ Rental of buildings, copiers, trucks and autos, telephone system equipment, and other assets.

♦ Wages, salaries, commissions, bonuses, and other compensation paid to managers, office staff, salespersons, warehouse workers, security guards, and other employees. (Compensation of production employees is included in the cost of goods manufactured and becomes part of inventory cost.)

♦ Payroll taxes and fringe benefit costs of labor, such as health and medical plan contributions by the employer and the cost of employee retirement plans (a difficult cost to measure for defined benefit plans but not so difficult for 401(k) and other types of defined contribution plans).

- Office and data processing supplies.

- Telephone, fax, Internet, and website costs.

- Inventory shrinkage due to shoplifting and employee theft or careless handling and storage of products; the cost of goods stolen and damaged may be recorded in the cost of goods sold expense or, alternatively, classified as an operating expense.

- Liability, fire, accident, and other insurance costs.

- Utility costs of electricity and fuel.

- Advertising and sales promotion costs, which are major expenditures by many businesses.

- Bad debts, which are past-due accounts receivable that turn out to be not collectible and have to be written off.

- Transportation and shipping costs.

- Travel and entertainment costs.

This list is not all-inclusive. We're sure you could think of many more expenses of operating a business. Even relatively small businesses keep 100 or more separate accounts for specific operating expenses. Larger business corporations keep thousands of specific expense accounts. In their external financial reports, however, most publicly owned corporations report only one, two, or three operating expenses. For instance, advertising expenses are reported internally to managers, but you don't see this particular expense in many external income statements.

As we mention earlier some operating expenses are recorded when they are paid—not before, nor after. The business records an expense and decreases cash. This chapter focuses on another basic way that operating expenses are recorded—by increasing the accounts payable liability. (Following chapters explain other ways of recording operating expenses and the asset and liability accounts involved.)

It would be convenient if every dollar of operating expenses were a dollar actually paid out in the same period. But, as this and later chapters demonstrate, running a business is not so simple. The point is that for many operating expenses a business cannot wait to record the expense until it pays the expense. As soon as a liability is incurred, the amount of expense should be recorded. The term *incurred* means that the business has a definite responsibility to pay a third party, outside the business.

A liability is incurred when a company takes on an obligation to make future payment and has received the economic benefit of the cost in operating the business. Recording the liability for an unpaid expense is one fundamental aspect of *accrual-basis accounting*. Expenses are *accrued* (i.e., recorded before they are paid) so that the amount of each expense is deducted from sales revenue in order to measure profit correctly for the period. You may want to quickly review Chapter 3 that explains recording expenses (and profit accounting in general).

For an example, suppose on December 15 a business receives an invoice from its attorneys for legal work done for the company over the previous two or three months. The end of the company's accounting (fiscal) year is December 31. The company will not pay its lawyers until next year. This cost belongs in this year, and should be recorded in the legal expense account. Therefore, the company records an increase in the accounts payable liability account to record the legal expense.

This is just one example of many; other examples include bills from newspapers for advertisements that have already appeared in the papers, telephone bills, and so on. Generally speaking, liabilities for unpaid expenses are for short credit periods, typically one month or less.

Based on its experience, a business should know the average time it takes to pay its short-term accounts payable arising from unpaid operating expenses. The average credit period of the company in our example is three weeks. Thus, the amount of its accounts payable from this source can be expressed as follows:

$$\frac{3}{52} \times \begin{array}{c} \$12{,}480{,}000 \\ \text{Operating Expenses} \\ \text{for Year} \end{array} = \begin{array}{c} \$720{,}000 \\ \text{Accounts} \\ \text{Payable} \end{array}$$

In Exhibit 8.1 note that the year-end amount for this component of accounts payable is $720,000.

Operating costs that are not paid immediately are recorded in the accounts payable liability account both to recognize the obligation of the business to make payment for these costs, and to record expenses that have benefited the operations of the business so that profit is measured correctly for the period. In other words, there is both an income statement and a balance sheet reason for recording unpaid expenses.

There's no question that accounts payable should be recorded for expenses that haven't been paid by the end of the accounting year. However, the recording of unpaid expenses does not immediately decrease cash. Actual cash outflow occurs later, when the accounts payable are paid. Chapter 3 briefly introduces of the cash flows side of revenue and expenses. Chapter 14 is a comprehensive explanation of the cash flow aspects of making profit and the statement of cash flows.

Accounting Issues

At the end of Chapter 7 we discuss the accounting issues regarding reporting accounts payable in the balance sheet. You may want to quickly review those points.

Generally speaking, there are no accounting problems regarding the accounts payable liability for unpaid operating expenses. The amounts that should be recorded are clear in most situations. The business receives invoices (bills) for these expenses that are definite regarding the amounts owed by the business. Some of its vendors and suppliers may offer prompt payment discounts. For example, the business may deduct 2 percent if it pays the bill in 10 days or sooner. Generally, a business adopts a standard way of dealing with such discounts and follows the method consistently.

The most contentious financial reporting issue concerns disclosure of operating expenses in a company's income statement. Suppose you were one of the stockholders in the business. Would you be satisfied with the company disclosing only one grand total for all its selling, general, and administrative expenses, as in Exhibit 2.2? Or would you want more detail?

In later chapters we discuss the broad issue of adequate disclosure in financial reports. All we'll say here is that financial reporting standards are not very demanding regarding disclosure of expenses in income statements to share owners. Companies can be tight-lipped if they so choose.

9

OPERATING EXPENSES AND PREPAID EXPENSES

EXHIBIT 9.1—SELLING, GENERAL, AND ADMINISTRATIVE EXPENSES AND PREPAID EXPENSES

Dollar Amounts in Thousands

ASSETS

Cash	$ 3,265
Accounts Receivable	$ 5,000
Inventory	$ 8,450
Prepaid Expenses	$ 960
Property, Plant, and Equipment	$16,500
Accumulated Depreciation	$ (4,250)
Intangible Assets	$ 5,575
Total Assets	$35,500

INCOME STATEMENT FOR YEAR

Sales Revenue	$ 52,000
Cost of Goods Sold Expense	$(33,800)
Selling, General, and Administrative Expenses	$(12,480)
Depreciation Expense	$ (785)
Interest Expense	$ (545)
Income Tax Expense	$ (1,748)
Net Income	$ 2,642

Assuming the business has paid certain costs that will not be recorded as expenses until next year that in total equals four weeks of its annual operating expenses, the year-end balance of Prepaid Expenses is:

$$4/52 \times \$12,480 = \$960$$

LIABILITIES AND STOCKHOLDERS' EQUITY

Accounts Payable	$ 3,320
Accrued Expenses Payable	$ 1,515
Income Tax Payable	$ 165
Short-Term Notes Payable	$ 3,125
Long-Term Notes Payable	$ 4,250
Capital Stock	$ 8,125
Retained Earnings	$15,000
Total Liabilities and Stockholders' Equity	$35,500

Paying Certain Operating Costs before They Are Recorded as Expenses

Please refer to Exhibit 9.1 at the start of the chapter, which highlights the connection between *selling, general,* and *administrative expenses* in the income statement and the *prepaid expenses* asset account in the balance sheet. This chapter explains that operating expenses drive this particular asset of a business.

The preceding chapter explains that some operating expenses are recorded before they are paid—by recording a liability for the unpaid expenses. This chapter, in contrast, explains that certain operating costs are paid *before* the amounts should be recorded as expenses. In short, businesses have to prepay some of their expenses.

Insurance premiums are one example of prepaid expenses. Insurance premiums are paid in advance of the insurance policy period—which usually extends over 6 or 12 months. Another example is office and computer supplies bought in bulk and then gradually used up over several weeks or months. Annual property taxes may be paid at the start of the tax year; these amounts should be allocated over the future months that benefit from the property taxes.

Cash outlays for prepaid costs are initially recorded not in an expense account but rather in the *prepaid expenses* asset account that acts as a holding account. Then the amounts are gradually charged out over time to operating expenses. This two-step process is the means of delaying the expensing of costs to future months. The prepaid cost is allocated so that each future month

receives its fair share of the cost. When the time comes, an entry is recorded to remove the appropriate portion of the cost from the prepaid expenses asset account, and the amount is entered in an operating expense account. (Chapter 3 shows the entry for removing cost out of the asset account into the expense account.)

Based on its experience and the nature of its operations, a business knows how large, on average, the total of its prepaid expenses is relative to its annual operating expenses. In this example the company's prepaid expenses equal four weeks of its annual operating expenses. Thus, the balance in its prepaid expenses asset account can be expressed as follows:

$$\frac{4}{52} \times \begin{array}{c} \$12{,}480{,}000 \text{ Selling,} \\ \text{General, and Administrative} \\ \text{Expenses for Year} \end{array} = \begin{array}{c} \$960{,}000 \\ \text{Prepaid} \\ \text{Expenses} \end{array}$$

In Exhibit 9.1, notice that the year-end balance of this asset account is $960,000. Its balance is much smaller than the company's balances of accounts receivable and inventory. (This is typical for most businesses.)

Summing up, the main reason for recording operating costs that are paid in advance in the prepaid expenses asset account is to delay recording these costs as expenses until the proper time. Charging off prepayments immediately to expenses would be premature—it would be robbing Paul (expenses higher this period) to pay Peter (expenses lower next period).

The main purpose of putting prepaid operating costs into the prepaid expenses account is not to recognize an asset, although prepaid costs are a legitimate asset. In one sense, prepaying an operating expense is similar to making an investment in a long-term operating asset such as a building, or equipment and machinery. Charging off prepaid operating costs to expenses is done over a short time frame, whereas allocating the cost of a building to expense is spread out over many years (as the next chapter explains).

The prepayment of operating expenses decreases cash. Cash outflow takes place sooner than the expense is recorded. Chapter 3 explains the cash flow effect of an increase in the prepaid expenses asset account. (Cash flow is lower because of the increase.) Chapter 14 presents a comprehensive summary of the cash flow analysis of all expenses and sales revenue.

Accounting Issues: Using Prepaid Expenses to Massage the Numbers

In the large majority of situations there are no serious accounting problems concerning prepaid expenses. On the other hand, we can imagine an unusual situation in which the balance in a company's prepaid expenses asset account should be written down as a loss. For instance, a business may be on the verge of collapse, and its prepaid expenses may therefore have no future benefit and may not be recoverable. In order words, accounting for prepaid expenses assumes that the business will remain a going concern in the foreseeable future. (This key assumption is made in accounting for all assets, although an imminent threat of shutting down a business would affect different assets differently.)

So far we haven't talked about *accounting fraud* and *massaging the numbers*. This is as good a place as any to open up the discussion about these dark corners of accounting. Accounting fraud is also called *cooking the books*, and massaging the numbers is also called *earnings management*. There is no bright line separating accounting fraud and massaging the numbers. Generally speaking accounting fraud is much bigger and typically involves the falsification of sales and/or the failure to recognize the full amount of expenses.

Massaging the numbers can be viewed as "fluffing the pillows," to make the accounting numbers and especially bottom-line profit look a little better than it would by strictly adhering to the company's established accounting methods and procedures. Massaging the numbers is like driving a little over the speed limit.

Accounting fraud is like driving while drunk with serious risks to others.

The prepaid expenses asset, being a relatively small asset, is generally not an important element in accounting fraud. However, the prepaid expenses asset account could easily be used for the manipulation of expenses. For example, a business may not record certain prepaid costs; instead it could record the prepayments immediately to expense. Alternatively, a business could intentionally delay charging off certain prepaid costs to expenses, even though the expenses should be recorded in this period.

Accountants, being in charge of recording revenue and expenses, are involved in any manipulation of expenses (and also revenue). But they do not take the initiative on their own in massaging the numbers. A top-level manager, either directly or indirectly, instructs the accountant to come up with more (or less) profit for the period—by whatever means it takes. In doing so the accountant has to override established accounting procedures. Needless to say, this puts the accountant in an ethical dilemma. For that matter, the heavy-handed manipulation of accounting numbers could possibly be a criminal offense. The CPA auditor of a company's financial statements should discover any significant amount of accounting manipulation.

We discuss massaging the numbers and accounting fraud at greater length in Chapters 20 (accounting methods) and 21 (audits). We should point out one further thing here, that massaging the numbers for sales revenue and expenses affects both the income statement *and* the balance sheet. Manipulating the accounting numbers has a double-edged effect—both the income statement and the balance sheet include incorrect amounts.

Suppose, for instance, that some of the products in the company's ending inventory suffered uninsured damage during the year. The damaged products will be sold next year below cost. Accounting theory is clear. The loss should be recorded in the period the damage occurs. But suppose top management does not want to record the hit against profit this year. The loss can be more easily absorbed next year (they think).

So, assume that the accountant does not record the loss this year. Therefore, bottom-line profit in the income statement is too high. And, the amount of inventory in the balance sheet at the end of the year is too high. Furthermore, the retained earnings account in the balance sheet (which accumulates the profit recorded each year) is too high. Both financial statements contain deliberate errors.

Needless to say, business managers and accountants should have ethical qualms about massaging the numbers. But we can say without fear of contradiction that manipulating accounting numbers goes on all the time. Everyone condemns accounting fraud, but there is not nearly as much wrath about massaging the numbers. This is a dark corner of accounting that accountants do not like to talk about. It's like we all disapprove of lying, even though most of us do a little.

10

DEPRECIATION EXPENSE AND PROPERTY, PLANT, AND EQUIPMENT; INTANGIBLE ASSETS

BALANCE SHEET AT YEAR-END

ASSETS

Cash		$ 3,265
Accounts Receivable		$ 5,000
Inventory		$ 8,450
Prepaid Expenses		$ 960
Property, Plant, and Equipment	$ 16,500	
Accumulated Depreciation	$ (4,250)	$12,250
Intangible Assets		$ 5,575
Total Assets		$35,500

The costs of long-term operating assets (except land) are allocated to depreciation expense over the years of their estimated useful lives

INCOME STATEMENT FOR YEAR

Sales Revenue	$ 52,000
Cost of Goods Sold Expense	$(33,800)
Selling, General, and Administrative Expenses	$(12,480)
Depreciation Expense	$ (785)
Interest Expense	$ (545)
Income Tax Expense	$ (1,748)
Net Income	$ 2,642

The amount of depreciation expense is not recorded as a decrease in the asset account. Instead it is accumulated in a *contra* or *offset* account, called *Accumulated Depreciation.*

LIABILITIES AND STOCKHOLDERS' EQUITY

Accounts Payable	$ 3,320
Accrued Expenses Payable	$ 1,515
Income Tax Payable	$ 165
Short-Term Notes Payable	$ 3,125
Long-Term Notes Payable	$ 4,250
Capital Stock	$ 8,125
Retained Earnings	$15,000
Total Liabilities and Stockholders' Equity	$35,500

Brief Review of Expense Accounting

Financial statement accounting is concerned with the *timing* for recording expenses—to record expenses in the correct period, neither too soon nor too late. The two guiding principles for recording expenses are:

1. ***Match expenses with sales revenue:*** Cost of goods sold expense, sales commissions expense, and any other expense directly connected with making particular sales are recorded in the same period as the sales revenue. This is straightforward; all direct expenses of making sales should be matched against sales revenue. It would be foolhardy to put revenue in one period and the expenses of that revenue in another period. You agree, don't you?

2. ***Match other expenses with the period benefited:*** Many expenses are not directly identifiable with particular sales, such as office employees' salaries, rental of warehouse space, computer processing and accounting costs, legal and audit fees, interest on borrowed money, and many more. Nondirect expenses are just as necessary as direct expenses. But nondirect expenses cannot be matched with particular sales. Therefore, nondirect expenses are recorded in the period in which the benefit to the business occurs.

Chapter 3 explains that the recording of an expense involves the decrease of an asset or the increase of a liability. Chapter 6 explains the use of the inventory asset account to hold the cost of products that are manufactured or purchased until the goods are sold, at which time cost of goods expense is recorded and the inventory asset account is decreased. Chapter 8 explains the use of the accounts payable liability account to record unpaid costs that should be recorded as expenses in the current period. Chapter 9 explains the use of the prepaid expenses asset account to delay recording operating expenses until the proper time period.

This chapter explains that the costs of the long-lived operating assets of a business in theory should be recorded to expense over the span of their useful lives. These assets (with the exception of land) gradually lose their usefulness to a business over time. The allocation of the cost of a long-term operating asset to expense over the useful life of the asset is called *depreciation*. In accounting depreciation means the multiyear *allocation* of the costs of long-term assets.

Depreciation Expense

Please refer to Exhibit 10.1 at the start of the chapter, which shows the connections between *property, plant*, and *equipment* in the balance sheet and *depreciation expense* in the income statement, and from depreciation expense back to *accumulated depreciation* in the balance sheet. In brief, the costs of the company's long-term operating assets are allocated (in theory) over their estimated economic lives, and the periodic depreciation expense is accumulated in a separate contra (offset) account that is deducted from the cost of the assets.

The company in this example needs certain specialized machinery, equipment, and tools that are rented under multiyear lease contracts. Legally the business doesn't own leased assets. The monthly rents paid on these leases are charged to expenses. Leased assets are not reported in a company's balance sheet (unless the lease is essentially a method to finance the purchase of the asset). A company should disclose rental payment commitments of its long-term leases in the footnotes to its financial statements. (*Note*: Accounting rule-makers are currently considering a proposal to report most leases in the balance sheet as an asset with a corresponding liability for future rental payments.)

The company in our example owns long-term operating assets—a production plant and office building, furniture and fixtures, computers, delivery trucks, forklifts, and automobiles used by its salespersons. The business buys these assets, uses them for several years, and eventually disposes of them. Because of their long-term nature, accountants call them *fixed assets*, although this term is not used in the formal financial statements of a business.

The long-term operating assets owned by a business usually are grouped into one inclusive account for balance sheet reporting. One common title is *Property, Plant*, and *Equipment*, which we use. (A detailed breakdown of fixed assets may be disclosed in a footnote to the financial statements, or in a separate schedule.) At the end of its most recent year, the business reports that the total cost of its fixed assets (property, plant, and equipment) is $16,500,000—see Exhibit 10.1. This amount is the total of the original costs of its fixed assets, or how much they cost when the business bought them.

Fixed assets are used for several years, but eventually they wear out or lose their utility to a business. In short, these assets have a limited life span—they don't last forever. For example, delivery trucks may be driven 200,000 or 300,000 miles, but are replaced eventually.

The cost of a delivery truck, for instance, is prorated over the years of expected use to the business. How many years, exactly? A business has its experience to go on in estimating the useful lives of fixed assets. In theory, a business should make the most realistic forecast possible regarding how long each fixed asset will be used, and then spread the asset's cost over this life span. However, theory doesn't count for much on this score. Most businesses turn to the federal income tax code and regulations for the useful lives of their fixed assets, because these lives are permitted for calculating the depreciation expense amounts that can be deducted in their federal income tax returns.

In the federal income tax system, every kind of fixed asset is given a minimum life over which its cost can be depreciated. The cost of land is not depreciated, on grounds that land never wears out and has a perpetual life. (The market value of a parcel of real estate can fluctuate over time; and floods and earthquakes can destroy land—but that's another matter.)

The federal income tax permits (but does not require) *accelerated depreciation* methods. The term *accelerated* means two different things. First, for income tax, fixed assets can be depreciated over lives that are considerably *shorter* than their actual useful lives. For example, automobiles and light trucks can be depreciated over five years even though these fixed assets typically last longer than five years (except perhaps taxicabs in New York City). Buildings placed in service after 1993 can be depreciated over 39 years, but most buildings stand longer. In writing the income tax law, Congress decided that allowing businesses to depreciate their fixed assets faster than they actually wear out is good economic policy.

Second, accelerated means *front-loaded*; more of the cost of a fixed asset is depreciated in the first half of its useful life than in its second half. Instead of a level, uniform amount of depreciation expense year to year (which is called the *straight-line* method), the income tax law allows a business to deduct higher amounts of depreciation expense in the front (early) years and less in the back (later) years.

A business can reduce its taxable income in the early years of its fixed assets by choosing accelerated depreciation methods. But these effects don't necessarily mean it's the best depreciation method in theory or in actual practice. Accelerated depreciation methods, given the imprimatur of the income tax code, are very popular.

A business must maintain a depreciation schedule for each of its fixed assets and keep track of original cost and how much depreciation expense is recorded each year. Only cost can be depreciated. Once the total cost of a fixed asset has been depreciated, no more depreciation expense can be recorded. At this point, the fixed asset is fully depreciated even though it still may be used several more years.

In our company example, the depreciation expense for its most recent year is $785,000—see Exhibit 10.1. Its manufacturing and office building is being depreciated by the straight-line method; its other fixed assets (e.g., trucks, computers, equipment) are being depreciated according to an accelerated method.

The amount of depreciation expense charged to each year is quite arbitrary compared with most other operating expenses. The main reason is that useful life estimates are arbitrary. For a six-month insurance policy, there's little doubt that the total premium cost should be allocated over exactly six months. But long-lived operating assets such as office desks, display shelving, file cabinets, computers, and so on present much more difficult problems. Past experience is a good guide but leaves a lot of room for error.

Given the inherent problems of estimating useful lives, financial statement readers are well advised to keep in mind the consequences of adopting ultraconservative useful life estimates. If useful life estimates are too short (the assets are actually used many more years), then depreciation expense is recorded too quickly. Keep this point in mind.

A business could keep two sets of depreciation books. It could depreciate fixed assets over short lives for income tax, and use longer, more realistic lives for financial reporting. However, most businesses use the income tax depreciation lives in their financial statements. Rapid (accelerated) depreciation is the norm in financial reporting.

Recording depreciation expense does *not*—we repeat, does *not*—decrease cash; cash is not involved in recording depreciation. Rather, recording depreciation expense has the effect of decreasing a fixed asset. To understand this point, you have to understand the accumulated depreciation account, which we explain next.

Accumulated Depreciation and Book Value of Fixed Assets

The amount of depreciation each period is *not* recorded directly as a decrease in the fixed asset account. Yet, decreasing the asset account would seem to make sense because the whole point of depreciation is to recognize the wearing out of the fixed asset over time. So, why not decrease the fixed asset account?

Well, the universal practice throughout the accounting world is to accumulate depreciation expense in a companion account called *accumulated depreciation*. This account does what its name implies—it accumulates, period by period, the amounts recorded as depreciation expense. In Exhibit 10.1, notice that the balance in this account at the end of the company's most recent year is $4,250,000.

Compared to the $16,500,000 cost of its fixed assets, the accumulated depreciation balance indicates that the company's fixed assets are not very old. Furthermore, the company recorded $785,000 depreciation expense in its most recent year. At this clip, a little more than five years' depreciation has been recorded on its property, plant, and equipment (fixed assets).

As you see in Exhibit 10.1, the balance in accumulated depreciation is deducted from the original cost of fixed assets. In our business example, the $16,500,000 cost of fixed assets minus the $4,250,000 accumulated depreciation equals $12,250,000. Cost less accumulated depreciation is referred to as the *book value* of fixed assets.

Generally the entire cost of a fixed asset is depreciated, assuming the business holds on to the asset until the end of its depreciation life. In one sense, book value represents future depreciation expense, although a business may dispose of some of its fixed assets before they are fully depreciated. (And keep in mind that the cost of land, which is included in the property, plant, and equipment account, is not depreciated.)

Finally, remember that the $4,250,000 accumulated depreciation balance is the total depreciation that has been recorded during all years the fixed assets have been used. It's not just the depreciation expense from the most recent year.

Book Values and Current Replacement Costs

After recording depreciation expense for its most recent year, the book value of the company's long-term operating (fixed) assets is $12,250,000 (see Exhibit 10.1). Suppose that the business could determine the current replacement costs at the balance sheet date of the same exact fixed assets in the same used condition. (This might not be entirely realistic.)

Would you expect that the current market replacement costs would be exactly the same as the book values of the fixed assets? Chances are that the current replacement costs would be higher than the book value of the fixed assets—due to general inflation and the use of accelerated depreciation methods.

The original costs of fixed assets reported in a balance sheet are not meant to be indicators of the current replacement costs of the assets. Original costs are the amounts of capital invested in the assets that should be recovered through sales revenue over the years of using the assets in the operations of the business. Depreciation accounting is a cost-recovery-based method—not a mark-to-market method. In short, fixed asset accounting does not attempt to record changes in current replacement cost.

We should point out that business managers shouldn't ignore the current replacement values of their fixed assets. Fixed assets can be destroyed or damaged by fire, flooding, riots, terrorist acts, tornadoes, explosions, and structural failure. Quite clearly, business managers should be concerned about insuring fixed assets for their current replacement costs. However, in financial reporting a business does not write up the recorded value of its fixed assets to reflect current replacement costs. (There's no rule prohibiting the disclosure of the estimated current replacement costs of its fixed assets, but businesses don't do this.)

You see criticism of financial statement accounting on grounds that depreciation expense is based on the historical cost of fixed assets—instead of current replacement costs. Someday Congress might consider changing the income tax law to allow replacement-cost-basis depreciation (without taxing the gain from writing up fixed assets to their higher replacement costs). We don't see any evidence of Congress making such a radical change in the federal income tax.

We must admit, though, that anything is possible regarding fixed-asset depreciation within the federal income tax law. For instance, we would not be surprised if Congress were to change the useful lives of fixed assets for business income tax purposes—which Congress has done in the past. But Congress has not been willing to abandon the actual cost basis for fixed-asset depreciation.

Intangible Assets

So far in the chapter we have focused on the depreciation of *tangible* fixed assets. Many businesses invest in *intangible* assets, which have no physical existence. You can't see or touch these assets. For example, a business may purchase a valuable patent that it will use in its production process over many years. Or a business may buy an established trademark that is well known among consumers. When a business buys patents or trademarks, the costs of these particular assets are recorded in long-term asset accounts called *Patents* and *Trademarks*.

A business may purchase another going business as a whole and pay more than the sum of its identifiable assets (minus its liabilities). Often the company to be acquired has been in business for many years and it has built up a trusted name and reputation. It may have a large list of loyal customers that will continue to buy the company's products in the future. The experience and loyalty of the acquired company's employees may be the main reason to pay for more than the identifiable assets being acquired in the purchase of the business. Or the business being bought out may have secret processes and product formulas that give it a strong competitive advantage.

There are many reasons to pay more for an established, going-concern business than just the sum of its identifiable assets (minus the liabilities being assumed when buying the business). When a business pays more than the sum of the specific assets (less liabilities) of the business being acquired, the excess is generally recorded in the asset account called *goodwill*. Whether to systematically charge off the cost of goodwill and other intangible assets has been a vexing issue over the years. We won't bore you here with an extended discussion of the various arguments.

At the present time, accounting standards do not require the systematic allocation of the cost of an intangible asset to expense (called *amortization* expense). Instead, when an intangible asset has suffered an observable loss of value, a business makes an entry to *write down* the recorded value of the intangible asset. Businesses make yearly assessments of whether their intangible assets have been impaired and, if so, record an expense for the effect of the impairment.

Based on its yearly assessment, the business in our example determined that its intangible assets did not suffer a loss of value during the year. Therefore it did not record an expense for its intangible assets. Notice in Exhibit 10.1 that there is no line of connection from the intangible assets account in the balance sheet to an expense in the income statement. Keep in mind, however, that an expense is recorded when there is a diminishment in value of a company's intangible assets.

Accounting Issues

There's a multitude of accounting problems regarding the depreciation of long-term operating assets, as well as other accounting problems concerning fixed assets. A company's fixed assets are typically a sizable part of its total assets, so these accounting problems are important.

Many books have been written on the theory of depreciation, arguing the merits of different methods. As we mention in the chapter, most businesses resort to the income tax ground rules for depreciating their fixed assets. This is a practical and expedient answer to depreciation accounting questions.

A business should write down a fixed asset if its economic value has become impaired. An airline, for example, could have surplus jets that it no longer needs, or a manufacturer may shut down an entire plant because of a fall-off in demand for the products made in the plant. When a business has excess capacity, it should take a hard look at whether its fixed assets should be written down. Making write-downs of fixed assets due to loss of economic value is painful, and can put a big dent in profit, of course.

There are accounting problems in drawing the line between the costs of routine maintenance of fixed assets, which should be expensed as you go, versus major outlays that extend the life or improve the appearance or efficiency of fixed assets. The costs of major improvements should be recorded in the fixed asset account and depreciated over future years.

A business may self-insure some of its fixed assets, instead of buying casualty insurance coverage, making it vulnerable to huge write-offs if it suffers an actual loss. When a business self-insures its fixed assets, should it record an estimated expense each year for a future loss that hasn't yet happened, and may never happen? Most businesses do not.

In summary, there are many serious accounting problems surrounding fixed assets. Therefore, a business definitely should explain its depreciation and other fixed asset accounting policies in the footnotes to its financial statements. Also, a company should disclose how it accounts for its intangible assets, especially when it makes a major write-down in one or more of these assets during the year.

In Chapter 6 we argue that the company's cost of goods sold expense accounting method should be consistent with how the business sets sales prices. Likewise, we would argue that choosing the depreciation expense method should be guided mainly by the number of years over which the business plans to recoup the costs invested in its fixed assets through sales revenue. If the business adopts a sales pricing policy for recapturing the cost of a fixed asset over, say, 20 years, we would argue that a 20-year depreciation life should be used. But it may depreciate the cost over 10 years, as permitted by the income tax law. Talk about a mismatch between sales revenue and expenses!

11

ACCRUING THE LIABILITY FOR UNPAID EXPENSES

EXHIBIT 11.1—ACCRUING UNPAID EXPENSES
Dollar Amounts in Thousands

Assuming six weeks of the year's total of selling, general, and administrative expenses is unpaid at year-end the amount payable for these operating expenses is: 6/52 x $12,480 = $1,440

A small amount of the annual interest expense is unpaid at year-end, which is recorded to recognize the full amount of interest expense for the year.

BALANCE SHEET AT YEAR-END

ASSETS

Cash	$ 3,265
Accounts Receivable	$ 5,000
Inventory	$ 8,450
Prepaid Expenses	$ 960
Property, Plant, and Equipment	$16,500
Accumulated Depreciation	$ (4,250)
Intangible Assets	$ 5,575
Total Assets	$35,500

INCOME STATEMENT FOR YEAR

Sales Revenue	$ 52,000
Cost of Goods Sold Expense	$(33,800)
Selling, General, and Administrative Expenses	$(12,480)
Depreciation Expense	$ (785)
Interest Expense	$ (545)
Income Tax Expense	$ (1,748)
Net Income	$ 2,642

LIABILITIES AND STOCKHOLDERS' EQUITY

Accounts Payable		$ 3,320
Accrued Expenses Payable	$1,440	
Accrued Expenses Payable	$ 75	$ 1,515
Income Tax Payable		$ 165
Short-Term Notes Payable		$ 3,125
Long-Term Notes Payable		$ 4,250
Capital Stock		$ 8,125
Retained Earnings		$15,000
Total Liabilities and Stockholders' Equity		$35,500

Recording the Accrued Liability for Operating Expenses

Please refer to Exhibit 11.1 at the start of the chapter, which highlights the connections between *selling, general, and administrative expenses* in the income statement and the *accrued expenses payable* liability in the balance sheet, and between *interest expense* in the income statement and the same liability in the balance sheet. You get two for the price of one in this chapter. Both connections are based on the same idea—unpaid expenses at year-end are recorded so that the full, correct amount of expense is recognized in measuring profit for the year.

Chapter 8 explains that a business records certain expenses as soon as the bills (invoices) are received for these operating costs, even though it doesn't pay the bills until weeks later. This chapter explains that a business has to go looking for certain unpaid expenses at the end of the period. No bills or invoices are received for these expenses; they build up, or *accrue*, over time.

For instance, the business in our example pays its salespersons commissions based on their individual sales each month. Commissions are calculated at the end of each month, but are not paid until the following month. At year-end, the sales commissions earned for the final month of the year have not been paid. To record the increase in this expense, the company makes an entry in the liability account *accrued expenses payable*, which is a different sort of liability than accounts payable.

The accountant should know which expenses accumulate over time and make the appropriate calculations for these unpaid amounts at year-end. A business does not receive an invoice (bill) for these expenses from an outside vendor or supplier. A business has to generate its own internal invoices to itself, as it were. Its accounting department must be especially alert to which specific expenses need to be accrued.

In addition to sales commissions payable, a business has several other accrued expenses that should be recorded at the end of the period; the following are typical examples:

- Accumulated vacation and sick leave pay owed to employees, which can add up to a sizable amount.

- Partial-month telephone and electricity costs that have been incurred but not yet billed to the company.

- Property taxes that should be charged to the year, but the business has not received the tax bill by the end of the year.

- Warranty and guarantee work on products already sold that will be done in the future; the sales revenue has been recorded this year, so these postsale expenses also should be recorded in the same period to match all expenses with sales revenue.

Failure to record accrued liabilities for unpaid expenses could cause serious errors in a company's annual financial statements—liabilities would be understated in its balance sheet and expenses would be understated in its income statement for the year. A business definitely should identify which expenses accumulate over time and record the appropriate amounts of these liabilities at the end of the year.

In this example, the company's average gestation period before paying certain of its operating expenses is six weeks. Thus, the amount of its accrued operating expenses payable at the end of the year can be expressed as follows:

$$\frac{6}{52} \times \begin{array}{c} \$12,480,000 \text{ Selling,} \\ \text{General, and Administrative} \\ \text{Expenses for Year} \end{array} = \begin{array}{c} \$1,440,000 \\ \text{Accrued Expenses} \\ \text{Payable} \end{array}$$

See in Exhibit 11.1 that the ending balance of accrued expenses payable includes $1,440,000 for operating expenses. Is six weeks right for a typical business? Well, it's difficult to generalize from business to business. We'd say that six weeks is more or less average, but keep in mind that every business is different.

We might mention that it is not unusual that the ending balance of a company's accrued expenses payable is larger than its accounts payable for unpaid operating expenses. In our business example, the ending balance of its accounts payable for operating expenses is $720,000 (from Exhibit 8.1), which is only half as much as its $1,440,000 accrued expenses payable at the end of the year.

Speaking of accounts payable, some businesses merge accrued expenses payable with accounts payable and report only one liability in their external balance sheets. Both types of liabilities are noninterest-bearing. Both emerge out of the operations of the business, and from manufacturing or purchasing products. For this reason they are sometimes called *spontaneous liabilities*, which means they arise on the spot, not from borrowing money but from operating the business. Grouping both types of liabilities in one account is acceptable under financial reporting standards, although many companies report them separately.

The changes of accounts payable and accrued expenses can have significant impacts on cash flow, which we explain in Chapter 14. The changes in the balances of these two liabilities have cash flow impacts that are important to understand.

Bringing Interest Expense Up to Snuff

Virtually all businesses have liabilities for accounts payable and accrued expenses payable—which are part and parcel of carrying on its operations. And most businesses borrow money from a bank or from other sources that lend money to businesses. A note or similar legal instrument is signed when borrowing; hence, the liability account is called *notes payable*. Interest is paid on borrowed money, whereas no interest is paid on accounts payable (unless the amount is seriously past due and an interest penalty is added by the creditor). Notes payable always are reported separately and not mixed with noninterest-bearing liabilities.

Interest is a charge per day for the use of borrowed money. Each and every day that money is borrowed increases the amount of interest owed to the lender. The ratio of interest to the amount borrowed is called the *interest rate*, and is stated as a percent. Percent means "per hundred." If you borrow $100,000 for one year and pay $6,000 interest for the use of the money for one year, the interest rate is:

$6,000 Interest ÷ $100,000 Borrowed
= $6 Per $100, or 6.0% Annual Interest Rate

Interest rates are stated as annual rates, even though the term of a loan can be shorter or longer than one year.

Interest is reported as a separate expense in income statements. It's not the size of the interest expense, but rather the special nature of interest that requires separate disclosure. Interest is a *financial* expense, as opposed to operating expenses. Interest depends on how the business is financed, which refers to the company's mix of capital sources. The basic choice is between debt capital and equity (the generic term for all kinds of ownership capital).

You may ask: When is interest paid? It depends. On short-term notes (one year or less), interest is commonly paid in one amount at the maturity date of the note, which is the last day of the loan period, at which time the amount borrowed and the accumulated interest are due. On long-term notes payable (longer than one year), interest is paid semiannually, or possibly monthly or quarterly. In any case, on both short-term and long-term notes there is a lag or delay in paying interest. Nevertheless, interest expense should be recorded for all days the money has been borrowed.

The accumulated amount of unpaid interest expense at the end of the accounting period is calculated and recorded in an accrued expenses payable type of account. In Exhibit 11.1, accrued interest payable at year-end is the second component of the accrued expenses payable liability. In our example, the amount of unpaid interest expense at year-end is fairly small, only $75,000. Generally speaking, accrued interest payable is not reported as a separate liability in external financial statements, although there is no rule against it.

Accounting Issues

One accounting issue concerns what to include in interest expense. In addition to interest paid to lenders, borrowing involves other types of costs to the business, such as loan application and processing fees, so-called points charged by lenders, and other incidental costs such as legal fees. Generally, most businesses put such extra charges in an operating expense account. So, the interest expense in the income statement is just that—the interest on its debts for the period.

The larger accounting issue concerns the accrual of operating costs—and there are many such costs. We have to tell you that the accrual of the liability for unpaid expenses depends on the good faith of the business in doing the calculations of these amounts—many of which involve arbitrary estimates and forecasts. This step in the accounting process can be easily used for *massaging the numbers*. This pejorative phrase refers to the deliberate manipulation of amounts recorded for sales revenue and expenses in order to record a higher (or lower) amount of profit for the period. (See also our discussion of this unsavory topic in Chapter 9.)

All we can do here is caution you that some businesses lay a heavy hand on the amounts recorded in their sales revenue and expense accounts, in order to smooth profit year to year or to give the profit for the year an artificial boost. These companies do not disclose in their financial statements that they have manipulated their accounting numbers to nudge profit up (or down).

As we allude to earlier in the chapter, accrued interest payable usually is not reported as a separate liability in a company's year-end balance sheet. However, if this particular liability were large, it very well should be reported separately in the balance sheet. If a business is seriously behind in paying interest on its debts, the liability for unpaid interest should be prominently reported in its balance sheet, to call attention to this situation.

This last comment segues into the messy topic regarding how to present the financial statements of a business that is in serious financial trouble and is in default on its debt. One basic premise of financial statement accounting is the *going concern assumption*. The accountant assumes that unless there is clear evidence to the contrary, the business will continue to operate in a normal manner and will not be forced into involuntary termination and liquidation of its assets. When a company is in serious default on its debt obligations, the creditors have the right to enforce their claims and in the extreme case shut the business down.

To stave off the drastic effects from unpaid creditors who may force it to shut down, the business can file for bankruptcy protection. This is a complicated area of law, way beyond the scope of this book. If there is a serious threat of such legal actions by creditors against the business, the financial statements of the business should make full disclosure of its precarious financial situation.

12

INCOME TAX EXPENSE
AND ITS LIABILITY

EXHIBIT 12.1—INCOME TAX EXPENSE AND INCOME TAX PAYABLE

Dollar Amounts in Thousands

INCOME STATEMENT FOR YEAR

Sales Revenue	$ 52,000
Cost of Goods Sold Expense	$(33,800)
Selling, General, and Administrative Expenses	$(12,480)
Depreciation Expense	$ (785)
Interest Expense	$ (545)
Income Tax Expense	$ (1,748)
Net Income	$ 2,642

A relatively small amount of the income tax expense for the year is unpaid at year-end, which is recorded in the Income Tax Payable liability account.

BALANCE SHEET AT YEAR-END

ASSETS

Cash	$ 3,265
Accounts Receivable	$ 5,000
Inventory	$ 8,450
Prepaid Expenses	$ 960
Property, Plant, and Equipment	$16,500
Accumulated Depreciation	$ (4,250)
Intangible Assets	$ 5,575
Total Assets	**$35,500**

LIABILITIES AND STOCKHOLDERS' EQUITY

Accounts Payable	$ 3,320
Accrued Expenses Payable	$ 1,515
Income Tax Payable	$ 165
Short-Term Notes Payable	$ 3,125
Long-Term Notes Payable	$ 4,250
Capital Stock	$ 8,125
Retained Earnings	$15,000
Total Liabilities and Stockholders' Equity	**$35,500**

Taxation of Business Profit

Please refer to Exhibit 12.1 at the start of the chapter, which highlights the connection between *income tax expense* in the income statement and the *income tax payable* liability in the balance sheet. Chapter 3 explains the accounting entry for recording income tax expense. Income tax expense is increased and the income tax liability is increased. The liability account is decreased as cash payments are made (and cash is decreased). Typically, not all of the income tax expense for the year is paid by the end of the year. In this company example a small part of the company's total income tax expense for the year, which is based on its *taxable income* for the year, has not been paid at year-end. This remaining balance will be paid in the near future. The unpaid portion stays in the company's income tax payable liability account until paid.

The business in our example is *incorporated*; the business decided on this form of legal organization (instead of a partnership or limited liability company). A corporation, being a separate person in the eyes of the law, has several important advantages. However, profit-motivated business corporations have one serious disadvantage—they are subject to federal and state income tax on their profits, or, to be more accurate, they owe tax based on their *taxable income*, which is earnings before income tax.

The business in this example is a regular, or so-called C corporation. This type of income tax entity is subject to double taxation of business profit—first in the hands of the business corporation, and second in the hands of its stockholders (but only to the extent that net income after income tax is distributed as cash dividends to them). Other types of legal business entities avoid the double taxation feature, but all their annual taxable income passes through to their owners who have to include their respective shares of the company's taxable income with their other sources of taxable income.

The first point to keep in mind is that a business corporation must earn *taxable income* to owe income tax. The simplest way to pay no income tax is to have no taxable income, or to have a loss for tax purposes. A business wants to earn profit, but earning a profit comes with the burden of sharing pretax profit with Uncle Sam and with the states that levy a tax on business profit earned within their borders.

A second point to keep in mind is that there are many loopholes and options in the federal income tax code—to say nothing about state income tax laws—that reduce or postpone income tax. We're sure that you're aware of the complexity of the federal income tax law. That's an understatement, if we've ever heard one.

It takes thousands of pages of tax law to define taxable income. Most businesses use income tax professionals to help them determine their taxable income, and to advise them how to minimize the income taxes they must pay. In any one year, a business might take advantage of several different features of the tax code to minimize its taxable income for the year, or to shift taxable income to future years.

For our business example, we have to simplify. The business pays both federal and state income taxes based on its taxable income. Furthermore, we assume in the example that the accounting methods used to prepare its income statement are exactly the same methods used to determine its annual taxable income. In this example, the company's earnings before income tax is $4,390,000 (you can refer back to Exhibit 2.2 to check this). We assume that this amount is its taxable income for the year. As you see in Exhibit 12.1, the income tax is $1,748,000, which is about 40 percent of taxable income. Keep in mind that the business pays both federal and state income taxes.

The federal income tax law requires that a business make installment payments during the year so that close to 100 percent of its annual income tax should be paid by the end of the tax year. Actually, a relatively small fraction of the total annual income tax may not be paid by year-end without any penalty (although this can get very complicated).

The company in this example paid most of its income taxes during the year. At year-end it still owes the federal and state tax authorities only $165,000 of its annual income tax. The unpaid portion is reported in the *income tax payable* liability account, as you see in Exhibit 12.1.

The federal income tax law changes year to year. Congress is always tinkering with, or, shall we say, fine-tuning the tax code. Old loopholes are shut down; new loopholes open up. Tax rates have changed over time. For these reasons the fraction of annual income tax that is unpaid at year-end is hard to predict. However, if the year-end income tax liability were a large fraction of the income tax expense for the year, we'd advise you to take a closer look.

Accounting Issues

A business may opt to use certain accounting methods to determine its annual taxable income that are different from the accounting methods used to report sales revenue and expenses in its income statement. Financial reporting standards require that the amount of income tax expense in the income statement be consistent with the amount of earnings before income tax in the income statement. The idea is to recognize a "normal" amount of income tax expense relative to the sales revenue and expenses above the income tax expense line. This normal amount of income tax is deducted to determine bottom-line net income after income tax.

Suppose a business reports $10,000,000 earnings before income tax in its income statement, and that the normal income tax would be $3,500,000 on this amount of taxable income. However, the business uses different accounting methods for income tax, and its actual income tax owed for the year is only, say, $2,500,000. Suppose that this difference is only temporary and will eventually reverse itself such that in future years the business will owe more income tax than will be reported in its future income statements.

In this situation the business records the full $3,500,000 amount of income tax, even though it owes only $2,500,000 for the year. The additional $1,000,000 needed to get the income tax expense up to the full $3,500,000 normal amount is recorded in a *deferred income tax liability* account—on the grounds that sooner or later the business will have to pay the additional $1,000,000 to the government.

We should tell you that there are many other problems in reporting income tax expense and income tax liabilities in business financial statements. These topics are very technical and beyond the scope of this book.

A company's financial report should include a schedule reconciling the actual income tax owed for the year (based on taxable income for the year) with the normal income tax expense reported in the income statement. We regret to tell you that this is one of the most difficult schedules you'll find in financial reports.

Accounting for income tax expense is an example of the *conditional* and *tentative* nature of financial statements. The numbers reported in financial statements might seem to be the final word on profit performance for the year and financial condition at the end of the year. But, in fact, financial statements are always provisional and subject to later revision. (We discuss the subsequent restatements of financial statements in Chapter 20.)

The amount of income tax expense recorded for the year and the corresponding balance sheet liability are subject to revision after the close of the year. The Internal Revenue Service (IRS) may have disagreements with the income tax returns filed by the business. Indeed, the IRS may do a full-scale audit and have many disagreements.

Some businesses push the envelope in interpreting the income tax law for determining annual taxable income. Or, a business may play it straight in how it reads the law. Even so, the income tax law is complex and not clear-cut on many points. In short, there's always the possibility that the IRS may claim more income tax (or perhaps even make a refund).

13

NET INCOME AND RETAINED EARNINGS; EARNINGS PER SHARE (EPS)

EXHIBIT 13.1 — NET INCOME AND RETAINED EARNINGS; EARNINGS PER SHARE (EPS)

Dollar Amounts in Thousands

BALANCE SHEET AT YEAR-END

ASSETS

Cash	$ 3,265
Accounts Receivable	$ 5,000
Inventory	$ 8,450
Prepaid Expenses	$ 960
Property, Plant, and Equipment	$16,500
Accumulated Depreciation	$ (4,250)
Intangible Assets	$ 5,575
Total Assets	$35,500

INCOME STATEMENT FOR YEAR

Sales Revenue	$ 52,000
Cost of Goods Sold Expense	$(33,800)
Selling, General, and Administrative Expenses	$(12,480)
Depreciation Expense	$ (785)
Interest Expense	$ (545)
Income Tax Expense	$ (1,748)
Net Income	$ 2,642
Earnings per Share	$ 3.30

> Bottom-line profit, or net income increases the Retained Earnings owners' equity account. (This account is decreased by dividends paid to shareholders.)

LIABILITIES AND STOCKHOLDERS' EQUITY

Accounts Payable	$ 3,320
Accrued Expenses Payable	$ 1,515
Income Tax Payable	$ 165
Short-Term Notes Payable	$ 3,125
Long-Term Notes Payable	$ 4,250
Capital Stock (800,000 shares)	$ 8,125
Retained Earnings	$15,000
Total Liabilities and Stockholders' Equity	$35,500

Net Income into Retained Earnings

Exhibit 13.1 at the start of the chapter highlights the connection from *net income* in the income statement to *retained earnings* in the balance sheet, and from net income to a new piece of information that we show for the first time—*earnings per share* (EPS). This chapter explains that earning profit increases the retained earnings account. And, we introduce earnings per share (EPS).

Suppose a business has $10 million total assets and $3 million total liabilities (including both noninterest-bearing operating liabilities such as accounts payable and interest-bearing notes payable). Over the years, its owners invested $4 million capital in the business. Therefore, liabilities plus capital from owners provide a total of $7 million of the company's total assets. Where did the other $3 million of assets come from?

Assets don't just drop down like "manna from heaven." All assets have a source, and one job of accountants is to keep track of the sources of assets of the business. The source of the other $3 million of assets must be from profit the business earned but did not distribute—from *retained earnings*.

Two basic types of owners' equity accounts are needed for every business—one for capital invested by the owners and one for retained earnings. In our example the business is organized legally as a corporation, and it issues *capital stock shares* to its owners when they invest money in the business. As you see in Exhibit 13.1 the company uses the account called *Capital Stock* to record the investment of money by stockholders in the business.

Whenever a business distributes money to its owners, it must distinguish between returning capital they have invested in the business (which is not taxable to them) versus dividing profit among them (which is taxable). A business corporation is required to keep separate accounts for capital stock and retained earnings, as you see in Exhibit 13.1.

The income statement reports that the business earned $2,642,000 bottom-line profit, or net income for the year (see Exhibit 13.1). Chapter 3 explains that at the end of the period the amount of net income is recorded as an increase in the retained earnings account. The retained earnings account is so named because annual profit is entered as an increase in the account, and distributions to owners from profit are entered as decreases in the account.

During the year, the business paid $750,000 total cash dividends from net income to its stockholders. Therefore, its retained earnings increased only $1,892,000 during the year: [$2,642,000 net income − $750,000 dividends = $1,892,000 net increase in retained earnings]. At the end of the year, its retained earnings balance stands at $15,000,000, which is the cumulative result from all years the company has been in existence.

Notice in this example that the company has a relatively large retained earnings balance compared with its total assets and other balance sheet accounts. This signals that the business has been profitable in the past. However, we can't tell from the balance sheet whether the company suffered a loss one or more years in the past. By the way, if a company's losses over the years were larger than its profits, its retained earnings account would have a *negative* balance, which generally is called *accumulated deficit* or a similar title.

Many people, even some experienced business managers, are confused about what retained earnings refers to. They mistakenly imagine that retained earnings refers to a cache of cash that has been set aside. No, a thousand times no! The balance of the retained earnings account does not refer to any particular asset and certainly not to cash. Yet, we can see that the title of this balance sheet owners' equity account could mislead people into thinking that it refers to money that the business has squirreled away.

Perhaps the best way to reinforce the correct meaning of retained earnings is to rearrange the accounting equation to put emphasis on retained earnings:

$$\text{Assets} - \text{Liabilities} - \text{Capital Invested by Owners}$$
$$= \text{Retained Earnings}$$

In other words, if you subtract the amount of liabilities and capital invested by owners the remainder of assets must be attributable to earnings that have been retained in the business. In our business example the numbers (in thousands) are as follows:

$$\underset{\text{Assets}}{\$35,500} - \underset{\text{Liabilities}}{\$12,375} - \underset{\text{Capital Stock}}{\$8,125} = \underset{\text{Retained Earnings}}{\$15,000}$$

In short, the balance in retained earnings explains one source of the total assets of a business. Making profit and keeping it in the business has added $15,000,000 to the total assets of the business in our example. You must look in the asset section of the balance sheet to see which particular assets the business owns. You can't tell a thing about which assets the business has by looking at the balance of its retained earnings. You're on the wrong side of the balance sheet.

When a business retains some (or all) of its annual net income, the retained profit should be considered as an addition to the ongoing capital base of the business. Businesses do not generally go back and pay a dividend from prior years' profits—although when a business piles up a huge cash hoard and has no other investment uses for the money it may make a large distribution out of retained earnings. (Apple comes to mind here although a good part of what Apple did in 2013 involved buying back a large number of its capital stock shares, as well as paying a hefty dividend.)

Looking down the road to the end of a business—after closing its doors, liquidating all of its assets, and paying off all of its liabilities, the business would distribute its remaining cash balance to its shareowners. The first layer of this final cash distribution to its shareowners is return of the capital they invested in the business. The remaining amount would be the final dividend (which is taxable).

Earnings per Share (EPS)

Net income, the bottom line in the income statement, is the profit measure for the business as a whole. Earnings per share (EPS) is the profit measure for each ownership unit, or for each share of capital stock of a business corporation.

Suppose in our example that you own 16,000 shares, or exactly 2 percent of the 800,000 shares of capital stock issued by the business. Several years ago you purchased these shares by investing $120,000 in the business, when it was just starting up. You're one of the original stockholders. Your $120,000 capital investment divided by your 16,000 shares means that your cost is $7.50 per share. Later investors paid more per share.

We can tell this from the company's balance sheet (see Exhibit 13.1). The $8,125,000 balance in the company's capital stock account divided by the 800,000 capital stock shares outstanding works out to an average of more than $10 per share. The later investors paid more per share than you did.

Owning only 2 percent of the total capital stock shares outstanding, you are a passive, outside investor in the business. You do not participate actively in managing the company. Of course you're entitled to 2 percent of any cash dividends paid from profit, and you control 2 percent of the votes on matters that have to be put to a vote of stockholders.

As a stockholder you are provided a copy of the company's annual (and quarterly) financial reports. Needless to say, you're very interested in the company's profit performance. You could take the view that 2 percent of annual net income "belongs" to you, which is a $52,840 slice of the company's total $2,642,000 net income. This is your cut of the net income pie. Or you could look at earnings per share (EPS), which is net income divided by the average number of capital stock shares outstanding during the year. In this example, EPS for the year just ended works out to $3.30 per share. Relative to your $7.50 cost per share you're earning a handsome return on your original investment in the business.

Earnings per share (EPS) is an especially important number for *public* companies whose capital stock shares are traded on securities exchanges. In fact, public companies must report EPS at the bottom of their income statements. Nonpublic companies do not have to report EPS although they may elect to do so. But we don't think many do. We discuss EPS further in Chapter 18.

Here, we'll just mention that EPS plays the key role in putting a market value on a share of stock in a business. For example, suppose we offer to buy 1,000 of your shares. You might offer to sell them at 15 times the stock's $3.30 EPS, or $49.50 per share. We might not be willing to pay this price. In any case, it's an important point of reference. Earnings per share of public companies get a lot of attention in the press.

Accounting Issues

Accounting problems don't concern retained earnings as such but rather sales revenue and expenses that determine profit for the period, which we've explained over the last several chapters. If net income is incorrect, then the retained earnings amount is incorrect.

There are some technical aspects of retained earnings, which are beyond the scope of this book. By and large, the financial reporting of retained earnings is straightforward and noncontroversial. But reporting EPS is another matter altogether. There are several problems in calculating EPS. To start with, many companies have to report not just one, but two figures for EPS—one based on the actual number of stock shares outstanding (in the hands of shareowners) and a second EPS that includes additional shares that the business is potentially committed to issue in the future. Before we close the book on retained earnings we should briefly mention another component of owners' equity called *Other Comprehensive Income*. You see this in the financial reports of many public companies. This element of owners' equity is reported separately from retained earnings. It accumulates certain types of gains and losses recorded on the assets of a business. One example is gains and losses from changes in foreign exchange ratios that haven't yet been executed by the business but affect the value of certain of its assets.

You would think that all asset gains and losses should pass through the income statement. However, these special income and loss items bypass the income statement and are recorded directly in the owners' equity account, Other Comprehensive Income. The thinking behind this treatment is that these peculiar gains and losses should not be included in the calculation of net income.

Part Three

CASH FLOW

14

CASH FLOW FROM OPERATING (PROFIT-MAKING) ACTIVITIES

EXHIBIT 14.1—CASH FLOW FROM OPERATING (PROFIT-MAKING) ACTIVITIES

Dollar Amounts in Thousands

BALANCE SHEET	Start of Year	End of Year	Change
Assets			
Cash	$ 3,735	$ 3,265	$(470)
Accounts Receivable	4,680	5,000	320
Inventory	7,515	8,450	935
Prepaid Expenses	685	960	275
Property, Plant, and Equipment	13,450	16,500	3,050
Accumulated Depreciation	(3,465)	(4,250)	(785)
Intangible Assets	5,000	5,575	575
Total Assets	$31,600	$35,500	
Liabilities and Stockholders' Equity			
Accounts Payable	$ 2,675	$ 3,320	645
Accrued Expenses Payable	1,035	1,515	480
Income Tax Payable	82	165	83
Short-Term Notes Payable	3,000	3,125	125
Long-Term Notes Payable	3,750	4,250	500
Capital Stock	7,950	8,125	175
Retained Earnings	13,108	15,000	1,892
Total Liabilities and Stockholders' Equity	$31,600	$35,500	

STATEMENT OF CASH FLOWS FOR YEAR

Net Income—See Income Statement	$ 2,642	
Accounts Receivable Increase	(320)	
Inventory Increase	(935)	
Prepaid Expenses Increase	(275)	
Depreciation Expense	785	
Accounts Payable Increase	645	
Accrued Expenses Payable Increase	480	
Income Tax Payable Increase	83	
Cash Flow from Operating Activities		$3,105
Investments in Property, Plant, and Equipment	$(3,050)	
Investments in Intangible Assets	(575)	
Cash Flow from Investing Activities		(3,625)
Increase in Short-Term Notes Payable	$ 125	
Increase in Long-Term Notes Payable	500	
Issue of Additional Capital Stock Shares	175	
Cash Dividends Paid Shareholders	(750)	
Cash Flow from Financing Activities		50
Decrease in Cash During Year		$ (470)

Profit and Cash Flow from Profit: Not Identical Twins!

At this point we shift gears. Chapters 5 through 13 (except for Chapter 6) walk down the income statement. Each chapter explains how sales revenue or an expense is connected with its corresponding asset or liability. You can't understand the balance sheet too well without understanding how sales revenue and expenses drive many of the assets and liabilities in the balance sheet. (In Chapter 3 we explain the increases and decreases of assets and liabilities in the recording of revenue and expenses.)

This chapter is the first of two that explain the *statement of cash flows*, which is the third primary financial statement reported by businesses in addition to the income statement and balance sheet. Exhibit 14.1 at the start of the chapter presents the statement of cash flows for the business we have discussed since Chapter 1. Please take a moment to read down this statement. We'll make you a wager here. We bet you understand the second and third sections of the statement (*investing* activities and *financing* activities) much better than the first section (*operating* activities).

Exhibit 14.1 shows the balance sheets of the company at the start and end of the year and includes a column for changes in assets, liabilities, and stockholders' equity. This chapter focuses on the first section of the cash flows statement, which presents cash flow from the company's operating activities (i.e., its *profit-making* activities) during the year. As you know, a company's profit-making activities are reported in its income statement. The income statement is not needed here to explain the first section of the statement of cash flows. Cash flow from operating activities is driven by changes during the period in the balance sheet.

The main question on everyone's mind seems to be why profit doesn't equal cash flow. In this example, the company earned $2,642,000 net income over the year just ended. Why didn't earning this amount of profit generate the same amount of cash flow? The first section in the cash flows statement provides the answer to this question.

The last line in the first section is labeled "Cash Flow from Operating Activities" (see Exhibit 14.1). Frankly, this is not the best name in the world. We prefer to call it *cash flow from profit*. The term *operating activities* is accounting jargon for sales revenue and expenses, which are the profit-making activities or operations of a business. Much of the time we refer to this line as cash flow from profit, which is shorter and more descriptive, we think. In any case, from the cash flows statement we see that the company generated $3,105,000 cash flow from profit compared with its $2,642,000 net income for the year.

Business managers have a double duty—first to earn profit, and second to convert the profit into cash as soon as possible. Waiting too long to turn profit into cash reduces its value because of the time value of money. Business managers should be clear on the difference between profit reported in the income statement and the amount of cash flow from profit during the year. Creditors and investors also should keep an eye on cash flow from profit (operating activities) and management's ability to control this important number.

To get from net income to the cash flow result from net income, we have to make adjustments along the way. Each is caused by a change during the year in one of the company's operating assets and liabilities (i.e., the assets and liabilities directly involved in recording sales revenue and expenses). We look at these adjustments in the order shown in the company's statement of cash flows. (Data is from Exhibit 14.1 at the start of the chapter.)

Changes in Assets and Liabilities That Impact Cash Flow from Operating Activities

1. *Accounts receivable:* At year-end the company had $5,000,000 uncollected sales revenue, which is the ending balance of its accounts receivable. The $5,000,000 is included in sales revenue for determining profit. But the company did not receive this amount of cash from customers. The $5,000,000 is still in accounts receivable instead of cash at year-end. However, the company collected its $4,680,000 beginning balance of accounts receivable. The $4,680,000 collected minus $5,000,000 not collected results in a $320,000 negative impact on cash flow. See the first adjustment in the cash flow statement (Exhibit 14.1). If short, an increase in accounts receivable hurts cash flow from profit.

2. *Inventory:* Notice the rather large increase in the company's inventory during the year. This may or may not have been a smart business decision. Perhaps the business needed a larger inventory to meet higher sales demand, or maybe not. In any case, the $935,000 inventory increase has a negative impact on cash flow. The quickest way to explain this

is as follows. Inventory is an investment in products in the process of being manufactured and finished products being held for sale. Increasing an investment means putting more money in the investment. See the second adjustment in the cash flow statement. In short, an increase in inventory hurts cash flow from operating activities (the profit-making activities of the business).

3. *Prepaid expenses:* During the year, the company paid $960,000 for certain operating costs that will benefit next year, and therefore were not charged to expenses in the year. See the ending balance in the company's prepaid expenses account. The company paid $960,000 on top of its operating expenses for the year. But the company had $685,000 of prepaid expenses at the start of the year; these costs were paid last year and then charged to operating expenses in the year just ended. Taking into account both the beginning and ending balances in prepaid expenses, the company experiences only $275,000 drain on cash during the year. The $685,000 not paid minus $960,000 paid has a $275,000 negative impact on cash flow. See the third adjustment in the cash flow statement (Exhibit 14.1).

4. *Depreciation:* During the year the company recorded $785,000 depreciation expense, not by writing a check for this amount but by writing down the cost of its property, plant, and equipment. This write-down is recorded as an increase in the accumulated depreciation account, which is the contra or offset account deducted from the property, plant, and equipment asset account. These long-term operating assets are partially written down each year to record the wear and tear on them during every year of use. The company paid cash for the assets when it bought these long-term resources. The company does not have to pay for them

a second time when it uses them. In short, depreciation expense is not a cash outlay in the year recorded and therefore is a positive adjustment, or so-called add back for determining cash flow from profit. See the fourth adjustment in the cash flow statement.

The depreciation add back to net income can be explained another way. For the sake of argument here, assume all sales revenue had been collected in cash during the year. Part of this cash inflow from customers pays the company for the use of its long-term operating assets during the year. In a sense, the business "sells" a fraction of its fixed assets to its customers each year. In setting its sales prices, a business includes depreciation as a cost of doing business. So, each year a business recovers part of the capital invested in its fixed assets in cash flow from sales revenue. In short, the company in this example recaptured $785,000 of the investment in its property, plant, and equipment assets, which is a significant source of cash flow.

5. *Accounts payable:* The ending balance in the company's accounts payable liability reveals that manufacturing costs, product purchases, and operating expenses were not fully paid during the year. The ending balance in this liability relieved the company of making cash payments in the amount of $3,320,000 (again see Exhibit 14.1). Not paying these costs avoids cash outflow. Consider the other side of the coin, as well. The company started the year with $2,675,000 accounts payable. These liabilities were paid during the year. The $3,320,000 not paid minus $2,675,000 paid has a net $645,000 positive impact on cash flow. See the fifth adjustment in the cash flow statement.

6. *Accrued expenses payable:* This liability works the same way as accounts payable. The company did not pay $1,515,000

of its expenses during the year, which is the balance in this liability at the end of the year. But the company did pay the $1,035,000 beginning amount of this liability. The $1,515,000 not paid minus $1,035,000 paid has a net $480,000 positive impact on cash flow. See the sixth adjustment in the cash flow statement.

7. *Income tax payable:* At the start of the year, the business owed the tax authorities $82,000 on taxable income from the previous year. This amount was paid early in the year. At the end of the year, the business owed $165,000 of its income tax expense for the year; this amount was not paid. The net effect is that the company paid $83,000 less to the government than its income tax expense for the year. See the positive adjustment for the increase in income tax payable in the cash flow statement.

Summing up the seven cash flow adjustments to net income:

- Increases in operating assets cause decreases in cash flow from profit; and decreases in operating assets result in increases in cash flow from profit.

- Increases in operating liabilities help cash flow from profit; and decreases in operating liabilities result in decreases in cash flow from profit.

See in Exhibit 14.1 that the combined net effect of the seven adjustments is that cash flow from profit is $3,105,000, which is $463,000 more than profit for the year. This difference between cash flow and bottom-line profit is due to the changes in the company's operating assets and liabilities. In summary, the business realized $3,105,000 cash flow from its operating activities during the year. This source of cash flow is vital to every business.

A Quick Word about the Direct Method for Reporting Cash Flow from Operating Activities

The accounting profession's rule-making body in the United States, the Financial Accounting Standards Board (FASB), has expressed a preference regarding the reporting of cash flow from operating activities. You might be surprised that the format you see in Exhibit 14.1 is *not* the preferred method. What you see in Exhibit 14.1 is called the *indirect method* that uses changes in operating assets and liabilities to adjust net income, which leads down to cash flow from operating activities. Instead, the FASB prefers the *direct method* for this section of the statement of cash flows.

EXHIBIT 14.2—DIRECT METHOD FORMAT FOR REPORTING CASH FLOW FROM OPERATING ACTIVITIES IN THE STATEMENT OF CASH FLOWS

Dollar Amounts in Thousands

Sales Revenue	$51,680
Cost of Goods Sold Expense	(34,760)
Operating Expenses	(11,630)
Interest Expense	(520)
Income Tax Expense	(1,665)
Cash Flow from Operating Activities	$ 3,105

Exhibit 14.2 shows the *direct method* format for reporting cash flow from operating activities. The cash flow amounts from sales revenue and for expenses are presented "directly" in this format. The direct method format is supplemented with a schedule that summarizes the changes in operating assets and liabilities, pretty much the same way as the changes are presented by the indirect method shown in Exhibit 14.1.

Both formats report the same cash flow from operating activities. Although the FASB expresses a clear preference for the direct method, the large majority of businesses use the indirect method in their external financial reports (which the FASB permits). Because of its popularity, we use the indirect method for the statement of cash flows in our business example.

An Alternative View of Cash Flow and Cash Flow

You frequently see "cash flow" mentioned in the business and financial press. In reading news items and articles, often it's not clear what the reporter means by the term *cash flow*. Reporters usually don't offer definitions of the term as they are using it. When they do define cash flow, they don't necessarily mean the amount in the statement of cash flows called cash flow from operating activities. They often use some other measure of cash flow. So, be careful when reading an article that refers to cash flow.

One alternative definition of cash flow has become popular: earnings before interest, (income) tax, depreciation, and amortization (EBITDA). For our business example, EBITDA is determined as follows (dollar amounts in thousands from income statement):

Calculation of EBITDA for Our Example

Net Income	$2,642
+ Interest Expense	$ 545
+ Income Tax Expense	$1,748
+ Depreciation Expense	$ 785
= EBITDA	$5,720

This financial metric is not an accurate measure of cash flow because interest and income tax are certainly cash flow expenses. EBITDA is more an alternative measure for operating profit, one that strips away how the company is financed and taxed and removes depreciation and amortization (if the business records any amortization expense). We explain in Chapter 10 that determining the amount of annual depreciation to record is arbitrary and typically is not consistent with economic reality. EBITDA should be used just for the purpose at hand. In using this measure you should have a crystal-clear understanding that this alternative profit measure is not cash flow from operating activities. Cash flows for interest and income tax expenses are not taken into account, and other factors affecting cash flow are ignored as well.

Changes in accounts receivable, inventory, prepaid expenses, accounts payable, accrued expenses payable, and income tax payable are ignored by the EBITDA definition of cash flow and profit. If all these changes in operating assets and liabilities are relatively minor, then simply adding back depreciation (and amortization, if any) to net income might be acceptable as a cash flow measure. But typically these changes are significant and cannot be ignored.

A final warning: In some situations cash flow is pushed to the forefront and profit is pushed to the background. When a business's profit performance is lackluster or when a business reports a loss, the CEO may prefer to shift attention to cash flow (assuming cash flow is healthy). However, cash flow is not a substitute for profit. The oldest trick in the book is to divert attention from bad news to whatever good news you can find. Simply put, profit generates cash flow; cash flow does not generate profit.

Accounting Issues

Most financial statement readers have a good intuitive understanding of a balance sheet (assets, liabilities, and shareholders' equity), and they have a good intuitive understanding that profit equals sales revenue minus expenses. In contrast, most financial statement readers seem confused about cash flow from profit. They think that making profit means making money, and that cash increases the same amount as bottom-line profit. This is not true, however. Profit and cash flow are two different numbers, both of which are important in their own right.

We remind you that accountants are accrual basis people, not cash basis people. To most accountants accrual basis is second nature. Indeed, we've met accountants who have trouble understanding cash flow because they are so submerged in the accrual basis. As a matter of fact, we've seen CPAs who have trouble preparing a statement of cash flows.

In preparing financial reports, accountants should keep in mind that the readers generally have a more difficult time understanding the statement of cash flow as compared with the balance sheet and income statement. But we see little evidence of this in the actual reporting of cash flow statements. We have read countless statements of cash flows. Many are exceedingly complicated. It's not unusual to find a statement of cash flows of a public company that reports 30, 40, or more lines of information. Furthermore, it is impossible to reconcile all the items reported in the statement of cash flows with their corresponding assets and liabilities in the balance sheet.

We believe that businesses should provide a more readable statement of cash flows. It would be quite helpful if management provided a brief summary and discussion of the company's cash flows for the year. Instead, the large majority of businesses offer little or no comment regarding their cash flows. You can make some headway in reading the statement of cash flows, but that's about it. Even CPAs would have trouble doing a complete and thorough analysis of the cash flows statements of many companies.

15

CASH FLOWS FROM INVESTING AND FINANCING ACTIVITIES

EXHIBIT 15.1—CASH FLOWS FROM INVESTING AND FINANCING ACTIVITIES

Dollar Amounts in Thousands

BALANCE SHEET	Start of Year	End of Year	Change
Assets			
Cash	$3,735	$3,265	$(470)
Accounts Receivable	4,680	5,000	320
Inventory	7,515	8,450	935
Prepaid Expenses	685	960	275
Property, Plant, and Equipment	13,450	16,500	3,050
Accumulated Depreciation	(3,465)	(4,250)	(785)
Intangible Assets	5,000	5,575	575
Total Assets	$31,600	$35,500	
Liabilities and Stockholders' Equity			
Accounts Payable	$2,675	$3,320	645
Accrued Expenses Payable	1,035	1,515	480
Income Tax Payable	82	165	83
Short-Term Notes Payable	3,000	3,125	125
Long-Term Notes Payable	3,750	4,250	500
Capital Stock	7,950	8,125	175
Retained Earnings	13,108	15,000	1,892
Total Liabilities and Stockholders' Equity	$31,600	$35,500	

STATEMENT OF CASH FLOWS FOR YEAR		
Net Income—See Income Statement	$2,642	
Accounts Receivable Increase	(320)	
Inventory Increase	(935)	
Prepaid Expenses Increase	(275)	
Depreciation Expense	785	
Accounts Payable Increase	645	
Accrued Expenses Payable Increase	480	
Income Tax Payable Increase	83	
Cash Flow from Operating Activities		$3,105
Investments in Property, Plant, and Equipment	$(3,050)	
Investments in Intangible Assets	(575)	
Cash Flow from Investing Activities		(3,625)
Increase in Short-Term Notes Payable	$125	
Increase in Long-Term Notes Payable	500	
Issue of Additional Capital Stock Shares	175	
Cash Dividends Paid Shareholders	(750)	
Cash Flow from Financing Activities		50
Decrease in Cash During Year		$ (470)

Rounding Out the Statement of Cash Flows

Please refer to Exhibit 15.1 at the start of the chapter. The preceding chapter explains the first of the three sections in the statement of cash flows, which without doubt is the hardest to understand. This chapter explains the other two sections of the cash flows statement, which are a piece of cake to understand compared with the first section that reports cash flow from operating activities.

The second section of the statement of cash flows (see Exhibit 15.1) summarizes the *investment activities* of the business during the year in long-term operating assets. In the example, the business spent $3,050,000 for new fixed assets (tangible long-term operating assets). See the line extending from this expenditure in the statement of cash flows to the property, plant, and equipment asset account in the balance sheet. In addition, the business increased its investment in intangible assets $575,000 during the year.

The investing activities section also includes proceeds from disposals of investments (net of tax), if there are any such disposals during the period. In our example, the business did not dispose of any of its long-term operating assets during the year—tangible or intangible. We should mention in passing that an ongoing business normally makes some disposals of fixed assets during the year.

The third section of the statement of cash flows (see Exhibit 15.1 again) reports the cash flows of *financing activities*. The term *financing* refers to dealings between the business and its sources of capital (i.e., its lenders and its stockholders). The business in our example increased its short-term and long-term debt during the year. It also raised a relatively small amount of $175,000 from issuing new capital stock shares (to key officers of the business). See the lines of connection from the statement of cash flows to the corresponding balance sheet accounts in Exhibit 15.1.

The business distributed $750,000 cash dividends from profit to its shareowners during the year. Cash dividends are included in the financing activities section of the cash flows statement. You may logically ask: Why not put cash dividends from profit next to cash flow from profit (i.e., from operating activities)? We say more about the placement of cash dividends later in the chapter. Its $2,642,000 net income for the year increases the company's retained earnings account (see Chapter 13), and the $750,000 cash dividends decreases the shareholders' equity account. Therefore, the net increase in retained earnings during the year is $1,892,000 (see Exhibit 15.1).

The bottom line of the statement of cash flows is the $470,000 decrease in cash during the year (see Exhibit 15.1). Well, perhaps we shouldn't call the change in cash the *bottom line*. The accounting authorities would not be amused. The term *bottom line* is more or less reserved for the last line of the income statement. But we see nothing wrong with referring to the bottom line of the cash flows statement. That line is the final, net result of all three types of activities that determine the increase or decrease in cash during the year.

Seeing the Big Picture of Cash Flows

Earning profit is a vital source of cash inflow to every business. Profit is the *internal* source of cash flow—money generated by the business itself without going outside the company to external sources of capital. Chapter 14 explains that the company generated $3,105,000 cash flow during the year just ended from its profit-making (operating) activities. Profit provided more than $3 million of money for the business, and this isn't chicken feed.

The obvious question is: What did the business do with its cash flow from profit? The remainder of the cash flows statement answers this important question. The rest of the cash flows statement reports other sources of cash that were tapped by the business during the year that provided additional capital to the business. And, most important, the statement of cash flows reveals what the business did with all this money.

From its profit-making activities the company generated $3,105,000 cash during the year. What *could* it do with this money? (We look at what it actually did in just a moment.) One option is simply to increase its cash balance—just let the money pile up in the company's checking account. This is not a productive use of the cash, unless the business is on the ragged edge and desperately needs to increase its day-to-day working cash balance. The business could also pay down some of its liabilities. Or the company could use some of the money to pay cash dividends to its stockholders.

In fact, the business did pay $750,000 cash dividends to its stockholders during the year. The amount of cash dividends to shareholders is one of the key items reported in the statement of cash flows—see the third section of the cash flows statement in Exhibit 15.1. After subtracting $750,000 cash dividends from the $3,105,000 cash flow from profit, the company had $2,355,000 cash flow remaining from operating activities. You may ask: What did the business do with this cash?

To modernize and expand its production and sales capacity, during the year the business invested $3,625,000 in new long-term operating assets including tangible and intangible assets (see Exhibit 15.1 again). These cash outlays are called capital expenditures, to emphasize the long-term nature of investing capital in these assets. You may have noticed that the total amount of capital expenditures was considerably more than cash flow from profit net of cash dividends ($3,625,000 capital expenditures less $2,355,000 cash flow from profit net of cash dividends equals $1,270,000 shortfall). This money had to come from somewhere.

A business has three sources to cover such a cash shortfall: (1) borrow more money on short-term and long-term debt; (2) secure additional capital from shareowners by issuing new capital stock shares; and (3) spend down its cash balance. The business in our example did some of all three, as seen in the following summary (amounts from Exhibit 15.1):

Cash Sources Used to Provide Amount Spent on Capital Expenditures during Year in Excess of Cash Flow from Operating Activities Net of Cash Dividends

Increase of short-term debt	$125,000
Increase of long-term debt	$500,000
Issue of additional capital stock shares	$175,000
Decrease in cash balance	$470,000
Total	$1,270,000

When a business is growing year to year, its cash flow from profit net of cash dividends usually does not provide all the cash it needs for its capital expenditures. Therefore, the business has to expand its debt and equity capital, which the business did in our example. Chapter 16 examines the impact of business growth and decline on cash flow from operating activities.

Business managers, lenders, and investors keep a close watch on capital expenditures. These cash outlays are a bet on the future by the company. The business is saying, in effect, that it needs the new fixed assets to maintain or improve its competitive position, or to expand its facilities for future growth. These are some of the most critical decisions business managers make.

Making capital investments is always risky. On one hand, who knows what will happen in the future? On the other hand, not making such investments may sign the death warrant of a business. By not making such investments, the company may fall behind its competition and lose market share that would be impossible to regain. Then again, being overinvested and having excess capacity can be an albatross around the neck of a business.

In any case, the business laid out $3,625,000 during the year for new assets (see Exhibit 15.1 again). In doing so, the business had to make key financing decisions—where to get the money for the asset purchases. As already mentioned, the business decided it could allow its working cash balance to drop $470,000. The company's ending cash balance is $3,265,000, which relative to its $52,000,000 annual sales revenue equals about three weeks of sales revenue.

We should point out that there are no general standards or guidelines regarding how large a company's working cash balance should be. Most business managers would view the company's cash balance in this example as adequate, we think. Just how much cash cushion does a business need as a safety reserve to protect against unfavorable developments?

What if the economy takes a nosedive, or what if the company has a serious falloff in sales? What if some of its accounts receivable are not collected on time? What if the company is not able to sell its inventory soon enough to keep the cash flow cycle in motion? What if it doesn't have enough money to pay its employees on time? There are no easy answers to these cash dilemmas.

The business could have forgone cash dividends in order to keep its working cash balance at a higher level. In all likelihood, its stockholders want a cash dividend on their investments in the business, and the board of directors was under pressure to deliver cash dividends. In any case, the business distributed $750,000 cash dividends, which are reported in the financing activities section in the cash flows statement (Exhibit 15.1).

In summary, the cash flows statement deserves as much attention and scrutiny as the income statement and balance sheet. Though not too likely, a company making a profit could be headed for liquidity problems (having too little ready cash) or solvency problems (not being able to pay liabilities on time). Profit does not guarantee liquidity and solvency. The cash flows statement should be read carefully to see if there are any danger signs or red flags.

At the end of Chapter 14 we mention that statements of cash flows reported by most public corporations are cluttered with a lot of detail—often far too much detail, in our opinion. One could get the impression that companies are deliberately making their cash flow statements hard to read, though this view may be too cynical.

Our advice is to focus mainly on the big-ticket items and skip the smaller details in reading a statement of cash flows. Stand back and try to see the big picture. The income statements reported by most public corporations have far fewer lines of information compared with cash flows statements and are generally much easier to understand. This is an odd state of affairs indeed.

Accounting Issues

There are several technical accounting problems in reporting cash flows. For example, should the cash flows connected with the discontinued operations of a business be reported separately from its ongoing, recurring cash flows? Should cash flows of certain short-term activities be reported gross or net? These cash flow issues are beyond the scope of this book. (We can almost hear you breathing easier here.)

One thing comes across loud and clear in the authoritative pronouncement on reporting cash flows. A business should not include cash flow per share in its financial reports. In particular, a business should not report cash flow from operating activities per share. You might recall from Chapter 13 that public companies are required to report earnings (net income) per share (EPS). The accounting authorities do not want financial statement readers to confuse EPS with cash flow.

One of our criticisms of the statement of cash flows—aside from the huge number of lines reported by most companies in this financial statement—is the placement of cash dividends in the financing activities section of the statement. Instead, we favor placing cash dividends immediately under cash flow from operating activities. Deducting the amount of cash dividends from cash flow from operating activities would highlight the amount of cash flow the company had available for general business purposes.

The purpose is to show more clearly how much of the cash flow from profit was available to the business after cash dividends. The financial statement reader could easily size up dividends against the amount of cash flow from profit, and see the amount of cash remaining for other needs of the business. But the current standard is to put dividends in the financing activities section of the cash flows statement. Our view is that businesses should have more options regarding where to place cash dividends in their statements of cash flows.

16

GROWTH AND DECLINE IMPACTS ON CASH FLOW

Setting the Stage

Chapter 16 explains how to get from net income (the bottom line of the income statement) to the cash flow yield from net income (which is found in the first section of the statement of cash flows). Cash flow almost always is higher or lower than net income for the period. There are three main reasons: (1) depreciation (and any noncash expenses and losses recorded in the period); (2) changes in operating assets; and, (3) changes in operating liabilities.

1. ***Depreciation (and noncash expenses and losses):*** Sales revenue reimburses a business for the expenses it incurs in making sales. Profit is the margin of sales revenue in excess of expenses. One expense is *depreciation*. A business records depreciation expense each period by writing down the cost balance of its property, plant, and equipment (except land). There is no cash outlay in recording this expense. Because depreciation is not a cash outlay the amount of the expense is an "add back" to net income for determining cash flow.

   In addition to depreciation, a business may record *noncash* expenses and losses. For example, a company may record *amortization* expense to recognize the loss of value of its intangible assets. Or, a business may record an uninsured loss that occurred during the year. Such asset write-downs do not involve a decrease in cash. Therefore, amortization expense and asset write-down losses are added back to net income (just like depreciation).

2. ***Operating assets:*** Changes in operating assets (accounts receivable, inventory, and prepaid expenses) affect cash flow from profit. An increase in accounts receivable means that less cash was actually collected than sales revenue for the period. Increases in operating assets require cash outflow to build up the assets. In contrast, a decrease in accounts receivable means that more cash was actually collected than sales revenue for the period. Decreases in other operating assets improve cash flow because the business, in effect, liquidates part of its investments in these operating assets.

3. ***Operating liabilities:*** Increases in operating liabilities (accounts payable, accrued expenses payable, and income tax payable) boost cash flow during the year. The business avoids cash outlay to the extent of the increases. In other words, part of total expenses for the year are not paid but are attributable to increases in these liabilities. Decreases in operating liabilities have the opposite effect: More cash is paid out than the amount of expenses for the year because the liabilities are paid down.

Caution: Simply adding back depreciation (plus any other noncash expenses and losses) to net income does not give you a true measure of cash flow from operating activities (profit). Changes in operating assets and liabilities during the year cause impacts on cash flow, which can be very sizable in some cases.

Cash Flows in the Steady-State Case

Let's look ahead to next year for the business example we have used throughout the book. In broad terms, the company's sales revenue next year will hold steady, grow, or decline. These are the three basic scenarios for next year. The scenarios have remarkably different impacts on cash flow from operating activities (cash flow from profit).

We start with the steady-state, or no-growth/no-decline scenario for the business example. Sales revenue and expenses in this scenario duplicate the year just ended. There are no changes. Exhibit 16.1 presents the first section of the company's cash flows

EXHIBIT 16.1—CASH FLOW FROM OPERATING (PROFIT-MAKING) ACTIVITIES IN STEADY-STATE SCENARIO
Dollar Amounts in Thousands

Net Income	$2,642
Accounts Receivable Change	0
Inventory Change	0
Prepaid Expenses Change	0
Depreciation Expense	785
Accounts Payable Change	0
Accrued Expenses Change	0
Income Tax Payable Change	0
Cash Flow from Operating Activities	$3,427

statement for next year for the steady-state situation. We don't bother to present its income statement for the coming year (it's a carbon copy of the one you've seen many times already).

Realistically, a company's sales revenue and expenses during the coming year will almost certainly change, at least a little bit. Our purpose here, however, is simply to provide a useful point of reference before moving on to the growth and decline scenarios.

In this example the company's accounts receivable equals five weeks of annual sales revenue, its inventory equals 13 weeks of annual cost of goods sold expense, and so on. These ratios can change over time. But in the steady-state scenario shown in Exhibit 16.1 all the operating ratios of sales revenue and expenses with their corresponding assets and liabilities are held constant for the coming year. The result is that you see zero changes for the company's operating assets and liabilities. The only adjustment to net income to determine cash flow is the depreciation add back.

We must admit that even in a steady-state situation the business may allow its average accounts receivable collection period to drift up, in which case its accounts receivable would increase. This increase would cause a negative cash flow adjustment to net income. Even when sales revenue and expenses remain constant the following year, a company's operating assets and liabilities may change because the average credit period extended to its customers may change, or its average inventory holding period may change, or its average credit period of accounts payable may change, and so on.

In our steady-state scenario cash flow from operating activities equals net income plus depreciation, which is $3,427,000 for the coming year. Cash flow from profit in a steady-state scenario is like milking a cow that gives a dependable, steady supply of cash flow every period, equal to depreciation (and other noncash items) plus net income. Indeed, the term *cash cow* is used to describe a business in a steady-state situation.

The $785,000 addition to cash flow from recapturing some of the capital invested in a company's fixed assets (the depreciation add back) provides a source of money for replacing fixed assets. Due to general inflation over the years, new fixed assets will probably cost more than the original cost of the fixed assets being replaced. To keep on a steady path, the business may have to use some of its cash flow from net income to replace fixed assets as they are retired.

Cash Flow Growth Penalty

Growth is the central strategy of many businesses. The purpose of growth is to increase profit and shareholders' wealth. Without good management, however, expenses can grow faster than sales revenue, and profit may actually decrease. In tough times, just holding its own may be the best a business can do.

Exhibit 16.2 presents a growth scenario for our business example in the coming year. The exhibit begins on the left with the income statement for the year just ended and shows the budgeted changes in sales revenue and expenses for the coming year. The company is planning for significant growth in sales revenue and profit next year. The CEO wants to know how this growth will impact the company's cash flow from profit next year. (We do not go into how the company arrived at its budgeted changes; we trust that the company's managers have done realistic forecasting and have set achievable goals for next year, which might not be entirely true.)

In Exhibit 16.2 the budgeted changes in sales revenue and expenses for the coming year are connected with their net income cash flow adjustments for next year. See the several lines of connection leading from the changes in the income statement into the cash flow from operating activities section of the cash flows statement.

The amounts of the changes in operating assets and liabilities assume that the company's operating ratios remain the same in the coming year. For instance, notice that cost of goods sold expense is budgeted to increase $4,225,000 next year. In our business

example, inventory equals 13 weeks of annual cost of goods sold. So, the increase in cost of goods sold expense causes the amount invested in inventory to increase accordingly:

$$\begin{array}{l}\text{\$4,225,000 Cost} \\ \text{of Good Sold} \\ \text{Expense Increase}\end{array} \times \frac{13}{52} = \begin{array}{l}\text{\$1,056,000} \\ \text{Inventory Increase} \\ \text{(Rounded)}\end{array}$$

In like manner, all other operating ratios in the business example are held constant in the growth scenario shown in Exhibit 16.2. Depreciation expense is not based on an operating ratio; rather, depreciation for the coming year is calculated from detailed schedules of the company's fixed assets (including new assets to be acquired in the coming year). This expense is budgeted to increase $95,000 next year because the company is planning to buy new fixed assets. Therefore, the depreciation add back to net income is $880,000 next year ($785,000 depreciation in year just ended + $95,000 increase in depreciation in coming year = $880,000 depreciation in coming year).

Profit is budgeted to increase $395,000 next year (see Exhibit 16.2), which equals a 15 percent increase over last year. The stockholders should be pleased. But if they anticipate that the business will also increase cash dividends 15 percent, they may be disappointed. Last year the business generated $3,105,000 cash flow from profit (from Exhibit 14.1). In the growth scenario, however,

EXHIBIT 16.2—CASH FLOW FROM OPERATING (PROFIT-MAKING) ACTIVITIES IN GROWTH SCENARIO
Dollar Amounts in Thousands

INCOME STATEMENT

	Actual Changes for Year Just Ended	Budgeted Changes for Next Year
Sales Revenue	$ 52,000	$ 6,500
Cost of Goods Sold Expense	33,800	4,225
Gross Margin	$ 18,200	
Selling, General, and Administrative Expenses	12,480	1,560
Depreciation Expense	785	95
Earnings before Interest and Income Tax	$ 4,935	
Interest Expense	545	35
Earnings before Income Tax	$ 4,390	
Income Tax Expense	1,748	190
Net Income	$ 2,642	$ 395
Budgeted Increase Next Year	$ 395	
Budgeted Net Income for Next Year	$ 3,037	

Budgeted Cash Flow from Operating Activities for Next Year	
Budgeted Net Income	$ 3,037
Accounts Receivable Increase	(625)
Inventory Increase	(1,056)
Prepaid Expenses Increase	(120)
Depreciation Expense	880
Accounts Payable Increase	415
Accrued Expenses Payable Increase	185
Income Tax Payable Increase	15
Cash Flow from Operating Activities	$ 2,731

notice that cash flow does *not* increase with the budgeted profit increase. Cash flow from profit is only $2,731,000 (see Exhibit 16.2). How do you like that?

The lower amount of cash flow from profit (compared with the year just ended) is caused by the rather large hits on cash flow resulting from the increases in accounts receivable and inventory next year that are needed to support the higher level of sales and expenses. These sizable negative cash flow adjustments to net income are offset to some extent by increases in operating liabilities. In short, profit goes up but cash flow from profit goes down!

There's no such thing as a free lunch for growth when it comes to cash flow. Growth should be good for profit next year, but growth almost always puts a dent in cash flow for the year. In other words, growth does not produce an instant cash flow increase equal to the increase in profit. Cash flow in all likelihood will decrease compared with the previous year—as it does in our business example.

Compare Exhibit 16.2, which shows $2,731,000 cash flow from profit for the growth scenario, with Exhibit 16.1, which shows cash flow from profit in the steady-state scenario. Cash flow is $3,427,000 in the steady-state case, or $696,000 higher. Profit is lower in the steady-state case, but cash flow is higher.

We don't mean to suggest that a business should sacrifice growth to keep its cash flow higher. We do want to make clear, however, that a business pays a cash flow penalty in the short run for growth. During a rapid growth phase, many companies suspend cash dividends to shareowners. All profit is "plowed back," or reinvested in the business.

A business could speed up cash flow from profit if it were able to improve its operating ratios, such as holding a smaller stock of products in inventory. However, improving operating ratios is generally very difficult in a period of growth. If anything, a business may be under pressure and allow its operating ratios to slip a little. For example, the company may offer customers more liberal credit terms to stimulate sales, which would extend the average accounts receivable credit period. Or the business may increase the size and mix of its inventory to improve delivery times to customers and to provide better selection.

Note: Exhibit 16.2 does not report the company's other sources of cash flow or how it plans to use its cash flow during the coming year. In other words, the *investing* and *financing* sections of the cash flow statement are not presented for the coming year. (Review Chapter 15 for an explanation of these cash flow sources and uses.) We don't see, for instance, how much the business is planning to spend on capital expenditures next year, or how much the company plans to distribute in cash dividends to its stockholders.

Cash Flow "Reward" from Decline

The old saying "what goes up must come down" certainly applies to most businesses. Few can keep growing forever; most high-growth businesses eventually slow down or reverse direction. There are cases of remarkable long-run sustained growth; Walmart comes to mind, for instance. But even stalwarts such as McDonald's have slowed down, leveled off, or declined. Some industries are cyclical by nature; their sales revenue goes up and down like a roller coaster over the business cycle.

Exhibit 16.3 presents the decline scenario. In our decline scenario cost of goods sold expense drops the same percent as sales revenue (which is realistic), and deprecation expense remains the same for the coming year on the grounds that the company would not immediately dispose of any fixed assets. As you should expect, profit performance suffers in a decline. It's difficult for a business to respond to a falloff in sales by cutting all its expenses immediately. For one thing, businesses are saddled with *fixed costs* that cannot be reduced in the short run when sales volume declines. A business has to carry out major surgery to reduce these fixed costs. What happens to cash flow from profit (operating activities) when a business suffers a decline in sales?

To illustrate the cash flow effect we keep the decrease in selling, general, and administrative expenses proportional with the decrease in sales revenue. But, to repeat, most businesses are saddled with fixed operating costs. A business may not be able to reduce its fixed costs right away when sales start to drop. The company needs more time to ratchet down its fixed costs.

In short, a company's expenses may not go down as quickly as sales.

The company's net income is budgeted to fall $450,000 in the decline scenario (see Exhibit 16.3 again). This is bad news. Net income would drop to $2,192,000. But cash flow from profit would be more than $4 million! You may find this rather surprising. In fact, you may even find this hard to believe. So, let us explain why.

In the decline scenario we assume that the company does not change any of its operating ratios. For example, the ratio of accounts receivable to annual sales revenue remains at five weeks. Since sales revenue drops $6,500,000, accounts receivable drops $625,000:

$$\begin{array}{ccc} \$6,500,000 & & \$625,000 \\ \text{Sales Revenue} \times \dfrac{5}{52} = & \text{Account Receivable} \\ \text{Decrease} & & \text{Decrease} \end{array}$$

In Exhibit 16.3 every operating asset and liability falls—including income tax payable because the business is budgeting a decrease in taxable income next year.

In most respects, the decline scenario (Exhibit 16.3) is just the flip side of the growth scenario (Exhibit 16.2). For example, in the growth scenario the $1,056,000 inventory increase is a negative adjustment to net income, but in the decline scenario the $1,056,000 inventory decrease is a positive adjustment to net income.

EXHIBIT 16.3—CASH FLOW FROM OPERATING (PROFIT-MAKING) ACTIVITIES IN DECLINE SCENARIO
Dollar Amounts in Thousands

INCOME STATEMENT

	Actual Changes for Year Just Ended	Budgeted Changes for Next Year
Sales Revenue	$52,000	$ (6,500)
Cost of Goods Sold Expense	33,800	(4,225)
Gross Margin	$ 18,200	
Selling, General, and Administrative Expenses	12,480	(1,560)
Depreciation Expense	785	0
Earnings before Interest and Income Tax	$ 4,935	
Interest Expense	545	(25)
Earnings before Income Tax	$ 4,390	
Income Tax Expense	1,748	(240)
Net Income	$ 2,642	$ (450)
Budgeted Increase Next Year	$ (450)	
Budgeted Net Income for Next Year	$ 2,192	

Budgeted Cash Flow from Operating Activities for Next Year	
Budgeted Net Income	$ 2,192
Accounts Receivable Decrease	625
Inventory Decrease	1,056
Prepaid Expenses Decrease	120
Depreciation Expense	785
Accounts Payable Decrease	(415)
Accrued Expenses Payable Decrease	(175)
Income Tax Payable Decrease	(45)
Cash Flow from Operating Activities	$ 4,143

In the decline scenario, the business would realize a substantial cash flow from profit and would have to decide what to do with the cash. The company could pay down its debt (interest-bearing liabilities), or possibly retire some of its capital stock shares. If the business predicts that the decline will be permanent, it should not need as much capital from debt and equity sources. At the lower level of sales, the company can get by on a lower level of assets, which means it needs less capital.

The broader challenge facing a business that suffers a serious downturn is developing a rebound strategy. Downsizing a business, particularly laying off employees who have been with the company many years, is painful for everyone. Downsizing means management has thrown in the towel and has given up on finding alternatives for maintaining the size of the business.

Red Ink and Cash Flow

Following our discussion of business decline in the preceding section, this is a good place to bring up an unpleasant subject. What happens to cash flow when the bottom line of the income statement is in red ink? In other words, what happens to cash flow when a business records a *net loss* for the year?

A net loss means that the total of expenses and losses is more than sales revenue (and income if any) for the year. Suppose a business records $10 million net loss for the year; did its cash decrease $10 million during the year? No, the cash impact from the net loss is bound to be different. To determine cash flow, you apply the same cash flow adjustments that are explained in Chapter 14. And, there is another factor to consider in many red ink cases.

A net loss for the year may be due to large write-downs of assets (or by recording a large liability). For example, the balance in a company's goodwill asset account may be written down because the asset suffered what is called *impairment*. This means that management has come to the conclusion that the asset has a lower future value to the business, or perhaps no value at all. The asset write-down does not involve a cash outlay. So, cash flow from operating activities is not hurt by such an asset write-down.

Suppose that a business records no asset write-downs (or liability write-ups) during the year, but reports a sizable net loss for the year. Its cash flow from operating activities could very well be negative. In other words, the total cash outlays for expenses could be more than total cash inflow from sales revenue, even after the depreciation add back. This condition is called *negative cash flow*.

In a negative cash flow situation, a business is using up its available cash. The rate at which the business is using up its cash is called the *burn rate*. The burn rate can be used to estimate how long the business can live without a major cash infusion. Start-up business ventures typically experience negative operating cash flow during their first few years. Often their burn rate remains too high and they don't make it.

Final Comment

Financial reporting standards do not require a business to explain or comment on its cash flow strategies and problems. The life or death of the business may be at stake, but top management may not say anything about how they expect to deal with their serious cash flow problems. Chapter 18 explains financial statement ratios that help lenders and investors identify liquidity and solvency problems of a business.

Part Four

ANALYSIS

17

FOOTNOTES TO FINANCIAL STATEMENTS

EXHIBIT 17.1—THREE FINANCIAL STATEMENTS AND FOOTNOTES

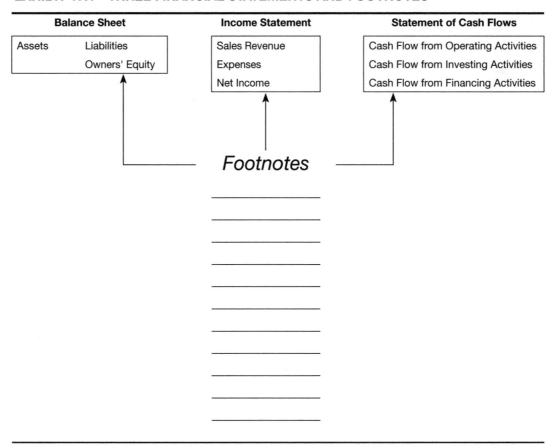

Balance Sheet	Income Statement	Statement of Cash Flows
Assets Liabilities Owners' Equity	Sales Revenue Expenses Net Income	Cash Flow from Operating Activities Cash Flow from Investing Activities Cash Flow from Financing Activities

Footnotes

This is the first of three chapters that discuss analyzing the information in business financial reports. This and the next chapter consider the information in *external* financial reports—those that circulate outside the business. These financial communications are designed mainly for the outside shareowners and lenders of the business, who are the two primary *stakeholders* in the business. The managers of a business have access to more information than released in the company's external financial reports. Chapter 19 discusses how managers can use the inside information for analyzing profit performance.

Exhibit 17.1 at the start of the chapter summarizes the principal elements of the three financial statements of a business and shows that *footnotes* are included with the three statements. Footnotes are the fourth essential part of every financial report. Financial statements would be "naked" without their footnotes. This chapter explains the importance of reading the footnotes and problems with footnotes. Studying a financial report should definitely include reading the footnotes to the financial statements.

Financial Statements—Brief Review

Before discussing footnotes, let's quickly review the three financial statements of a business that we explain in previous chapters.

1. **Balance sheet:** Also called the *statement of financial condition*, the balance sheet is a relative brief and condensed summary of a company's assets, liabilities, and owners' (stockholders') equity at the close of business on the last day of the income statement period. In reading a balance sheet, you need to understand the differences between basic types of assets (inventory versus property, plant, and equipment, for instance), and differences between operating liabilities (mainly accounts payable and accrued expenses payable) versus debt on which the business pays interest. Also, you should know the difference between the two different sources of owners' equity—capital invested by the owners in the business versus profit earned and not distributed to owners, which is called *retained earnings*.

2. **Income statement:** This financial statement summarizes a company's sales revenue and expenses for the period (the profit-making activities of the business), and it reports the company's bottom-line *net income* for the period, also called *earnings* and more popularly simply *profit*. A publicly owned business corporation must report its earnings per share

(EPS) with its income statement. A nonpublic company doesn't have to report earnings per share.

3. **Statement of cash flows:** Making a profit has cash flow effects. But, as we explain in Chapters 3 and 14, the amount of cash flow from making profit during the year does not equal bottom-line profit (net income) for the year. This financial statement divides cash flows into three groups. The first section provides a trail from net income to cash flow from *operating (profit-making) activities*. The second section summarizes the cash flow of the company's *investing activities* during the year. The third section summarizes the cash flow from the company's *financing activities* during the year. The statement of cash flows exposes the financial strategy of the business. For example, you can compare dividends paid during the year against its cash flow from operating activities (profit), which is a major financial decision of the business.

In short, the three financial statements report on the three financial imperatives facing every business—making a profit, remaining in healthy financial condition, and making good use of cash flow.

Most businesses—large and small, public and private—present comparative financial statements for their most recent two years or three years. This multiyear presentation allows financial statement readers to make comparisons between the year just ended and the preceding year, and the year before that. The federal agency that regulates financial reporting by public corporations, the Securities and Exchange Commission (SEC), requires three-year comparative financial statements.

According to various estimates, there are about 5,000 *public* companies in the United States. The financial reports of public companies are required to be audited annually by an independent certified public accountant (CPA) firm. The largest four international CPA firms (called the *Big Four*) audit the large majority of public companies. There are millions of *private* businesses in the United States. Private companies may or may not have their financial reports audited by an independent CPA firm. Generally, they are not legally required to have audits. We discuss financial report audits in Chapter 21.

Why Footnotes?

Without footnotes, financial statements would be incomplete, and possibly misleading. Footnotes are an essential *extension* to the three primary financial statements. Each financial statement is presented on one page, or at most two pages, in a financial report. Keep in mind that each financial statement is very condensed and presents highly compacted information.

It comes down to this: The lenders and investors in a business need more information than can be put into the financial statements. We suppose you could integrate this additional information into each financial statement. But can you imagine reading a balance sheet or an income statement that runs 5-, 10-, or 20-pages long? We don't think so. Therefore, the practical solution is to present the additional information in the form of supplementary footnotes to the financial statements. If you have a financial stake in the business you definitely should read the footnotes to its financial statements.

One overarching premise of financial reporting is *adequate disclosure*, so that all those who have a legitimate interest in the financial affairs of the business are provided the relevant information they need to make informed decisions and to protect their interests in the business. Footnotes are needed because the additional information provided in the footnotes is important to financial statement readers.

Top-level managers should not forget that they are responsible for the company's financial statements *and the accompanying footnotes*. The footnotes are an integral, inseparable part of a financial report. Financial statements state this fact on the bottom of each page, usually worded as follows:

The accompanying footnotes to the financial statements are an integral part of these statements.

The CPA auditor's report covers footnotes as well as the financial statements.

Ideally, footnotes should be written in an understandable manner, and every effort should be made to use language and visual layouts, schedules, and exhibits that are clear and reasonably easy to follow. In other words, financial reports should be *transparent*. The lack of transparency in financial reports has come in for much criticism, especially regarding footnotes that are so dense and obtuse that even a lawyer would have trouble reading them. More on this point later in the chapter.

Two Types of Footnotes

One type of footnote identifies and discusses the key accounting methods used by the business. As we discuss in Chapter 20, for several expenses and even for revenue a business can choose between two (or more) acceptable accounting methods. The company's selections of accounting methods should be made clear in its footnotes. A footnote is needed for each significant accounting choice by the business.

Here's an example of the types of accounting methods footnotes you find in financial reports (at least in the reports of public companies). In its 2012 financial report filed with the SEC Caterpillar included footnotes explaining its accounting methods for the following items (pages A11–A18):

- Nature of operations (machinery and power systems versus financial products).
- Basis of presentation (consolidation methods).
- Sales and revenue recognition (a detailed list).
- Inventories (use of the LIFO method and effects if the alternative FIFO method had been used).
- Depreciation and amortization.
- Foreign currency translations.
- Derivative financial instruments.
- Income taxes.

- Estimates in financial statements.
- New accounting guidelines (standards) that took effect in year.
- Goodwill.
- Accumulated other comprehensive income.
- Assets held for sale.

Caterpillar's footnotes occupy more pages than its financial statements themselves, which is not that unusual.

Warning: Footnotes assume that you are familiar with general accounting terminology. A business may be in an industry that is relatively unique and very different than most other businesses, in which case it might explain unusual terminology in its footnotes. But, by and large, companies do not include a glossary of accounting terms to help readers of their financial reports.

One of Caterpillar's footnotes explains how it goes about consolidating the various legal entities that make up the conglomerate entity called Caterpillar. Most large businesses consist of a family of corporations under the control of one parent company, which is the case for Caterpillar. The financial statements of each corporation are grouped together into one integrated set of financial statements. Intercorporate dealings are eliminated as if there were only one entity. Affiliated companies in which the business has made investments are not consolidated if the company does not have a controlling interest in the other business.

In addition to footnotes that identify accounting methods, footnotes are needed to provide important information that cannot be placed in the financial statements themselves. For example, the maturity dates, interest rates, collateral or other security provisions, and other details of the long-term debt of a business are presented in footnotes. Annual rentals required under long-term operating leases are given. Details regarding stock options and stock-based compensation plans are spelled out, and the dilution effects on earnings per share are illustrated in footnotes.

Major lawsuits and other legal actions against the company are discussed in footnotes. Details about the company's employees' retirement and pension plans are disclosed in footnotes. Obligations of the business to pay for postretirement health and medical costs of retired employees are presented in footnotes.

The list of possible footnotes is a long one. In preparing its annual report, a business needs to go down an exhaustive checklist of items that may have to be disclosed, and then actually write the footnotes. This is no easy task. The business has to explain in a relatively small space what can be rather complex.

Management Discretion in Writing Footnotes

Business executives have to rely on the experts—the chief financial officer of the organization, legal counsel, and the outside CPA auditor—to go through the checklist of footnotes that may be required. Once every required footnote has been identified, key decisions still have to be made regarding each footnote. A business has a good deal of discretion and latitude regarding just how candid to be and how much detail to reveal in each footnote.

Clearly, business managers should not give away the farm—they should not divulge information that would damage a competitive advantage that the business enjoys. Managers don't have to help their competitors. The idea is to help the company's creditors and stockholders—to report to them information they're entitled to.

But just how much information do the creditors and stockholders really need? How much are they legally entitled to? These are difficult questions to answer in straightforward and clear-cut terms. Beyond certain basic facts, exactly what should be put in a footnote to comply with the standard of adequate disclosure is not always clear and definite.

Too little disclosure, such as withholding information about a major lawsuit against the business, would be misleading, and the top executives of the business would be liable for such lack of disclosure. Beyond the legal minimum, which should be insisted on by the company's CPA auditors, footnote disclosure rules and guidelines are somewhat vague and murky.

Business executives, in fact, have rather broad freedom of choice regarding how frank to be and how to express what they put in footnotes. Quite clearly, footnotes are not written like newspaper articles. If the company's advertising copy were written like its footnotes, the business wouldn't make many sales.

Analysis Issues

Admittedly, we may be somewhat biased regarding footnotes to financial statements. Excuse us if we jump on the soapbox here. We see a very serious financial reporting problem regarding the readability of footnotes. As authors we may be overly sensitive to this, but we think not. Investors and securities analysts complain about the dense fog in footnotes. Footnote writing can be so obtuse that you have to suspect that the writing is deliberately obscure. The rules require footnotes, but the rules fail to demand that the footnotes be clear and concise so that an average financial report reader can understand them.

All too often the sentence structure of footnotes seems intentionally legalistic and awkward. Technical terminology abounds in footnotes. Poor writing seems more prevalent in footnotes on sensitive matters, such as lawsuits or ventures that the business abandoned with heavy losses. A lack of candor is obvious in many footnotes.

Creditors and stockholders cannot expect managers to expose all the dirty linen of the business in footnotes, or to confess all their bad decisions. But, better clarity and more frankness certainly would help and should not damage the business.

In short, creditors and investors often are stymied by poorly written footnotes. You have only one option, and that is to plow through the underbrush of troublesome footnotes, more than once if necessary. Usually you can tell if particular footnotes are important enough to deserve this extra effort. Beyond this advice, all we can say to you regarding reading footnotes is: "Good luck."

18

FINANCIAL STATEMENT RATIOS

Financial Reporting Ground Rules

The main purpose of external financial reporting is to provide up-to-date financial information from a business to its investors and lenders. The investors and lenders are its sources of capital and they have a right to and need for the information. Other parties are also interested in the financial affairs of a business—for example, its employees and its other creditors. When they read financial reports, they should keep in mind that these communications are directed to the owner-investors of the business and its lenders. External financial reporting standards have been developed with this primary audience in mind.

According to estimates, there are about 5,000 publicly owned businesses in the United States. Their capital stock shares and other securities are traded in public markets. The dissemination of financial information by these companies is governed by federal law, which is enforced mainly by the Securities and Exchange Commission (SEC). The New York Stock Exchange, Nasdaq, and Internet securities markets also enforce rules and regulations over the communication of financial information by companies whose securities are traded on their markets.

Securities of some 12,000 foreign businesses are traded in stock markets around the world. Many countries, including the United States, have been attempting to develop a set of *international financial reporting and accounting standards*. This process has not gone as smoothly as many had hoped for. Indeed, at this time (2013) the SEC has not yet given its formal endorsement of international standards. U.S. businesses are not yet required to adopt the global standards.

In the United States and other countries, a business cannot legally release information to some stockholders or lenders but not to others, nor can a business tip off some of them before informing the others. The laws and established standards of financial reporting are designed to ensure that all stockholders and lenders have equal access to a company's financial information and financial reports.

A company's financial report may not be the first source of information about its profit performance. In the United States, most public corporations issue press releases of their most recent earnings results. These press releases precede the mailing of hard copies of the company's financial report to its stockholders and lenders. Most public companies put their financial reports on their websites at the time of or soon after the press releases. Private businesses do not usually send out letters to their owners and lenders in advance of their financial reports, although they could. Private companies do not put their financial reports on publicly accessible websites.

This chapter examines what stockholders and lenders do with financial reports once they have access to them. The chapter centers on the *annual* financial report. (Quarterly financial reports are abbreviated versions of the annual reports.) In particular, this chapter focuses on certain *financial statement ratios* that are widely used by investors and lenders.

Financial Statement Preliminaries

Exhibit 18.1 presents a company's annual financial statements. This is the same company example used throughout earlier chapters. The footnotes for these statements are not included. (Chapter 17 discusses footnotes to financial statements.)

Our company example is privately owned, which means that its capital stock shares are not traded in a public market. The business has about 50 shareholders; some are managers of the business, including the CEO, the president, and several vice presidents. A business this size could go into the public marketplace for equity capital through an initial public offering (IPO) of capital stock shares and become publicly owned. However, the company has decided to remain private.

This chapter does not pretend to cover the field of *securities analysis* (i.e., the analysis of stocks and debt instruments issued by corporations). This broad field includes the analysis of competitive advantages and disadvantages of a business, domestic and international economic developments, business combination possibilities, general economic conditions, and much more. The key ratios explained in this chapter are basic building blocks in securities analysis.

Also, this chapter does not discuss *trend analysis*, which involves comparing a company's latest financial statements with its previous years' statements to identify important year-to-year changes. For example, investors and lenders are very interested in the sales growth or decline of a business, and the resulting impact on profit performance, cash flow, and financial condition. (Chapter 16 examines the impact of growth and decline on cash flow.)

This chapter has a more modest objective—to explain basic ratios used in financial statement analysis. Only a handful of ratios are discussed in the chapter, but they are fundamentally important.

On opening a company's financial report, probably one of the first things most investors do is to give the financial statements a once-over; they do a fairly quick scan of the financial statements. What do most financial report readers first look for? In our experience, they look first at the bottom line of the income statement, to see if the business made a profit or suffered a loss for the year.

As one sports celebrity put it when explaining how he keeps tabs on his various business investments, he looks first to see if the bottom line has "parentheses around it." The business in our example does not; it made a profit. Its income statement reports that the business earned $2,642,000 net income, or bottom-line profit for the year. Is this profit performance good, mediocre, or poor? Ratios help answer this question.

After reading the income statement, most financial statement readers probably take a quick look at the company's assets and compare them with the liabilities of the business. Are the assets adequate to the demands of the company's liabilities? Ratios help answer this question.

Extraordinary Gains and Losses

The business in our example does not report any *extraordinary gains or losses* for the year, which are one-time, nonrecurring

EXHIBIT 18.1—EXTERNAL FINANCIAL STATEMENTS OF BUSINESS (WITHOUT FOOTNOTES)

Dollar Amounts in Thousands, Except Earnings per Share

INCOME STATEMENT FOR YEAR

Sales Revenue	$ 52,000
Cost of Goods Sold Expense	33,800
Gross Margin	$ 18,200
Selling, General, and Administrative Expenses	12,480
Depreciation Expense	785
Earnings before Interest and Tax	$ 4,935
Interest Expense	545
Earnings before Tax	$ 4,390
Income Tax Expense	1,748
Net Income	$ 2,642
Basic Earnings per Share	$ 3.30

STATEMENT OF CHANGES IN STOCKHOLDERS' EQUITY FOR YEAR

	CAPITAL STOCK	RETAINED EARNINGS
Beginning Balances	$ 7,950	$ 13,108
Net Income for Year		2,642
Shares Issued During Year	$ 175	
Dividends Paid During Year		$ (750)
Ending Balances	$ 8,125	$ 15,000

BALANCE SHEET AT END OF YEAR

ASSETS

Cash		$ 3,265
Accounts Receivable		5,000
Inventory		8,450
Prepaid Expenses		960
Current Assets		$ 17,675
Property, Plant, and Equipment	$ 16,500	
Accumulated Depreciation	(4,250)	12,250
Intangible Assets		5,575
Total Assets		$ 35,500

Liabilities and Owners' Equity

Accounts Payable		$ 3,320
Accrued Expenses Payable		1,515
Income Tax Payable		165
Short-Term Notes Payable		3,125
Current Liabilities		$ 8,125
Long-Term Notes Payable		4,250
Total Liabilities		$ 12,375
Capital Stock (800,000 shares)	$ 8,125	
Retained Earnings	15,000	
Stockholders' Equity		$ 23,125
Total Liabilities and Stockholders' Equity		$ 35,500

STATEMENT OF CASH FLOWS FOR YEAR

Net Income	$ 2,642
Accounts Receivable Increase	(320)
Inventory Increase	(935)
Prepaid Expenses Increase	(275)
Depreciation Expense	785
Accounts Payable Increase	645
Accrued Expenses Payable Increase	480
Income Tax Payable Increase	83
Cash Flow from Operating Activities	$ 3,105
Expenditures for Property, Plant, and Equipment	$ (3,050)
Expenditures for Intangible Assets	(575)
Cash Flow from Investing Activities	(3,625)
Increase in Short-Term Notes Payable	$ 125
Increase in Long-Term Notes Payable	500
Issue of 7,000 Capital Stock Shares	175
Cash Dividends Paid Shareholders	(750)
Cash Flow from Financing Activities	50
Decrease in Cash During Year	$ (470)
Cash Balance at Start of Year	3,735
Cash Balance at End of Year	3,265

events. For example, a business may sell a major fixed asset and record a gain. Or a business may record a restructuring charge for the cost of laying off employees who will receive severance packages. These out-of-the-ordinary, unusual gains and losses are reported separately from the ongoing, continuing operations of a company. This topic would lead us into a labyrinth of technical details.

But be warned: These irregular gains and losses complicate the evaluation and forecasting of profit performance! Extraordinary gains and losses, especially losses, raise troublesome questions, such as:

- Is an extraordinary loss really a correction of past years' accounting mistakes?

- What if a company reports such irregular gains and losses on a recurring basis (instead of infrequently)?

- Will such extraordinary gains and losses be reported again in the future, and if so when and how much?

Deciding how to interpret and assess extraordinary gains and losses is a vexing challenge, to say the least.

No Cash Flow Ratios, But . . .

As you see, the company's statement of cash flows is included in Exhibit 18.1. This is one of the three primary financial statements of a business entity that is included in its external financial reports. Nevertheless, we almost didn't include it in the exhibit, which might surprise you.

None of the benchmark ratios discussed in this chapter involve the statement of cash flows—because no cash flow ratios have emerged or are in widespread use. Still, cash flow gets a lot of ink

in the financial press and in reports on corporations published by stockbrokers and investment advisors. Cash flow from profit (operating activities) is considered a key factor for all businesses.

The business in our example realized $3,105,000 net cash flow from profit (operating activities) for the year just ended. You could compare this important cash flow number with the company's $3,625,000 capital expenditures for the year (see Exhibit 18.1). As you see in its statement of cash flows the company's financing activities provided only $50,000 net cash inflow for the year. Thus, the company's cash balance dropped $470,000 during the year. None of these comparisons use ratios as such. But financial report readers should find such comparisons helpful for understanding the cash flow strategy of the business. Reading the cash flow statement in this manner provides a useful synopsis of where the business got its money during the year and what it did with the money.

We could divide cash flow from profit ($3,105,000) by net income ($2,642,000) to determine cash flow as a percentage of net income (118 percent). We think this is an interesting ratio. But it is not one of the benchmark ratios used in financial statement analysis (at least not yet).

We could divide cash flow from profit (operating activities) by the number of capital stock shares to get cash flow per share. The authoritative financial reporting standard setter in the United States, the Financial Accounting Standards Board (FASB), specifically discouraged this ratio, which is most unusual. It is quite rare for the FASB to go out of its way to put the kibosh on a particular ratio.

A New Financial Statement

Exhibit 18.1 introduces a new financial statement—the *statement of changes in stockholders' equity for year*—that we have not presented before in the book. In some respects this is not really a financial statement—it's more of a supporting schedule that summarizes changes in the stockholders' equity accounts. The business issued 7,000 additional shares of capital stock during the year. The $175,000 cash from issuing the shares are reported in the statement of changes in stockholders' equity as well as the statement of cash flows (see Exhibit 18.1). Net income for the year is reported as an increase in retained earnings, and cash dividends paid to stockholders as a decrease.

The statement of changes in stockholders' equity is definitely needed when a business has a capitalization (ownership) structure that includes two or more classes of stock, and when a business owns some of its own capital stock shares (called *treasury stock*). This financial statement is also needed when a business has recorded certain types of losses and gains that bypass the income statement. These special gains and losses are put in a special stockholders' equity account called *Accumulated Other Comprehensive Income*.

The term *comprehensive income* connotes that, in addition to net income that flows through the income statement into the retained earnings account, additional gains and losses have been recorded that have not been reported in the income statement. The accumulated other comprehensive income account serves like a second retained earnings type account, which holds the cumulative result of recording certain types of gains and losses. Exploring these special gains and losses would take us into a technical territory beyond the scope of this book.

Be warned: the statement of changes in stockholders' equity can be complex and highly technical. In the following discussion we focus on the most widely used ratios that are calculated from data in the big three financial statements (balance sheet, income statement, and statement of cash flows).

Benchmark Financial Ratios

Stock analysts, investment managers, individual investors, investment bankers, economists, and many others are interested in the fundamental financial aspects of a business. Ratios are a big help in analyzing the financial situation and performance of a business. So far in the book only two financial statement ratios have been mentioned: the *accounts receivable turnover ratio* in Chapter 5 and the *inventory turnover ratio* in Chapter 6. At this point you might be anticipating that we will begin with profit analysis. No, we start with *solvency*.

Solvency refers to the ability of a business to pay its liabilities when they come due. If a business is insolvent and cannot pay its liabilities on time its very continuance is a stake. In many respects solvency comes first and profit second. The ability to earn profit rests on the ability of the business to continue on course and avoid being shut down or interfered with by its lenders. In short, earning profit demands that a business remains solvent. Maintaining solvency (its debt-paying ability) is essential for every business. If a business defaults on its debt obligations, it becomes vulnerable to legal proceedings that could stop the company in its tracks, or at least could interfere with its normal operations.

Bankers and other lenders, when deciding whether to make and renew loans to a business, direct their attention to certain key financial statement ratios to help them evaluate the solvency situation and prospects of the business. These ratios provide a useful financial profile of the business in assessing its creditworthiness and for judging the ability of the business to pay interest and to repay the principal of its loans on time and in full.

Note: From here forward in the chapter all amounts from the financial statements are in thousands of dollars, except earnings per share (EPS). Instead of reminding you every time we assume that you remember that the relevant data is taken from Exhibit 18.1.

Current Ratio

The *current ratio* tests the short-term liability-paying ability of a business. It is calculated by dividing total current assets by total current liabilities in a company's most recent balance sheet. The current ratio for the company is computed as follows:

$$\frac{\$17,675 \text{ Current Assets}}{\$8,125 \text{ Current Liabilities}} = 2.18 \text{ Current Ratio}$$

The current ratio is hardly ever expressed as a percent (which would be 218 percent for this company example). The current ratio for the business is stated as 2.18 to 1.00, or more simply just as 2.18.

The common opinion is that the current ratio for a business should be 2 to 1 or higher. Most businesses find that their creditors expect this minimum current ratio. In other words, short-term creditors generally like to see a business limit its current liabilities to one-half or less of its current assets.

Why do short-term creditors put this limit on a business? The main reason is to provide a safety cushion of protection for the payment of the company's short-term liabilities. A current ratio of 2 to 1 means there is $2 of cash and assets that should be converted into cash during the near future that will be available to pay each $1 of current liabilities that come due in roughly the same time period. Each dollar of short-term liabilities is backed up with $2 of cash on hand or near-term cash inflows. The extra dollar of current assets provides a margin of safety for the creditors.

A company may be able to pay its liabilities on time with a current ratio less than 2 to 1, or perhaps even if its current ratio were as low as 1 to 1. In our business example, the company has borrowed $3,125,000 on the basis of short-term notes payable, which equals 18 percent of its total current assets. Its short-term lenders may not be willing to lend the business much more—although perhaps the business could persuade its lenders to go up to, say, $4 million or $5 million on short-term notes payable.

In summary, short-term sources of credit generally demand that a company's current assets be double its current liabilities. After all, creditors are not owners—they don't share in the profit earned by the business. The income on their loans is limited to the interest they charge (and collect). As creditors, they quite properly minimize their loan risks; as limited-income (fixed-income) investors, they are not compensated to take on much risk.

Acid Test Ratio (aka Quick Ratio)

Inventory is many weeks away from conversion into cash. Products are typically held two, three, or four months before being sold. If sales are made on credit, which is normal when one business sells to another business, there is a second waiting period before the receivables are collected. In short, inventory is not nearly as liquid as accounts receivable; it takes much longer to convert inventory into cash. Furthermore, there's no guarantee that all the products in inventory will be sold.

A more severe measure of the short-term liability-paying ability of a business is the *acid test ratio*, which excludes inventory (and prepaid expenses also). Only cash, short-term marketable securities investments (if any), and accounts receivable are counted as sources to pay the current liabilities of the business.

This ratio is also called the *quick ratio* because only cash and assets quickly convertible into cash are included in the amount available for paying current liabilities. It's more in the nature of a liquidity ratio that focuses on how much cash and near-cash assets a business possesses to pay all of its short-term liabilities.

In this example, the company's acid test ratio is calculated as follows (the business has no investments in marketable securities):

$$\frac{\$3,265 \text{ Cash} + \$5,000 \text{ Accounts Receivable}}{\$8,125 \text{ Current Liablities}} = 1.02 \text{ Acid Test Ratio}$$

The general rule is that a company's acid test ratio should be 1 to 1 or better, although you find many exceptions.

Debt to Equity Ratio

Some debt is generally good, but too much debt is dangerous. The *debt to equity ratio* is an indicator of whether a company is using debt prudently, or perhaps has gone too far and is overburdened with debt that may likely cause problems. For this example, the company's debt to equity ratio calculation is:

$$\frac{\$12,375 \text{ Total Liabilities}}{\$23,123 \text{ Total Stockholders Equity}} = .54 \text{ Debt to Equity Ratio}$$

This ratio tells us that the company is using $.54 of liabilities in addition to each $1 of stockholders' equity in the business. Notice that all liabilities (noninterest-bearing as well as interest-bearing, and both short term and long term) are included in this ratio, and that all owners' equity (invested capital stock and retained earnings) is included.

This business—with its .54 debt to equity ratio—would be viewed as moderately leveraged. *Leverage* refers to using the equity capital base to raise additional capital from nonowner sources. In other words, the business is using $1.54 of total capital for every $1 of equity capital. The business has $1.54 of assets working for it for every dollar of equity capital in the business.

Most businesses stay below a 1 to 1 debt to equity ratio. They don't want to take on too much debt, or they cannot convince lenders to put up more than one-half of their assets. However, some capital-intensive (asset-heavy) businesses such as public utilities and financial institutions operate with debt to equity ratios much higher than 1 to 1. In other words, they are highly leveraged.

Times Interest Earned Ratio

To pay interest on its debt, a business needs to have sufficient earnings before interest and (income) tax (EBIT). To test the ability to pay interest from earnings, the *times interest earned ratio*

is calculated. Annual earnings before interest and income tax is divided by interest expense:

$$\frac{\$4,935 \text{ EBIT}}{\$545 \text{ Interest Expenses}} = \frac{9.1 \text{ Times Interest}}{\text{Earned Ratio}}$$

There is no standard or general rule for this particular ratio—although obviously the ratio should be higher than 1 to 1. In this example, the company's EBIT is more than nine times its annual interest expense, which is comforting to its lenders. Lenders would be alarmed if a business barely covers its annual interest expense. (The company's management and stockholders should be equally alarmed.)

Return on Sales Ratio

Making sales while controlling expenses is how a business makes profit. The profit residual slice from a company's total sales revenue pie is expressed by the *return on sales ratio*, which is profit divided by sales revenue for the period. The company's return on sales ratio for its latest year is:

$$\frac{\$2,642 \text{ Net Income}}{\$52,000 \text{ Sales Revenue}} = 5.1\% \text{ Return on Sales Ratio}$$

There is another way of explaining the return on sales ratio. For each $100 of sales revenue, the business earned $5.10 net income—and had expenses of $94.90. Return on sales varies quite markedly from one industry to another. Some businesses do well with only a 2 percent return on sales; others need more than 10 percent to justify the large amount of capital invested in their assets.

Return on Equity (ROE)

Owners take the risk of whether their business can earn a profit and sustain its profit performance over the years. How much would you pay for a business that consistently suffers a loss? The value of the owners' investment depends first and foremost on the past and potential future profit performance of the business—or not just profit, we should say, but profit relative to the capital invested to earn that profit.

For instance, suppose a business earns $100,000 annual net income for its stockholders. If its stockholders' equity is $250,000, then its profit performance relative to the stockholders' capital used to make that profit is 40 percent, which is very good indeed. If, however, stockholders' equity is $2,500,000, then the company's profit performance equals only 4 percent of owners' equity, which is weak relative to the owners' capital used to earn that profit.

In short, profit should be compared with the amount of capital invested to earn that profit. Profit for a period divided by the amount of capital invested to earn that profit is generally called *return on investment* (ROI). ROI is a broad concept that applies to almost any sort of investment of capital.

The owners' historical investment in a business is the total of the owners' equity accounts in the company's balance sheet. Their profit is bottom-line net income for the period—well, maybe not all of net income. A business corporation may issue *preferred stock* on which a fixed amount of dividends have to be paid each year. The preferred stock shares have the first claim on dividends from net income. Therefore, preferred stock dividends are subtracted from net income to determine the *net income available for the common stockholders*. In this example the business has issued only one class of stock shares. The company has no preferred stock, so all of net income "belongs" to its common stockholders.

Dividing annual net income by stockholders' equity gives the *return on equity* (ROE) ratio. The calculation for the company's ROE in this example is:

$$\frac{\$2,642 \text{ Net Income}}{\$23,125 \text{ Stockholders' Equity}} = \frac{11.4\% \text{ Return}}{\text{on Equity Ratio}}$$

Note: We use the ending balance of stockholders' equity to simplify the calculation. Alternatively, the weighted average during the year could be used, and should be if there have been significant changes during the year.

By most standards, this company's 11.4 percent annual ROE would be acceptable but not impressive. However, everything is relative. ROE should be compared with industrywide averages and with investment alternatives. Also, the risk factor is important: Just how risky is the stockholders' capital investment in the business?

We need to know much more about the history and prospects of the business to reach a final conclusion regarding whether its 11.4 percent ROE is good, mediocre, or poor. Also, we should consider the *opportunity cost of capital*—that is, the ROI the stockholders could have earned on the next best use of their capital. Furthermore, we have not considered the personal income tax on dividends paid to its individual stockholders. In summary, judging ROE is not a simple matter!

Return on Assets (ROA)

Here's another useful profit performance ratio:

$$\frac{\$4,935 \text{ EBIT}}{\$35,500 \text{ Total Assets}} = \frac{13.9\% \text{ Return on}}{\text{Assets Ratio}}$$

The *return on assets* (ROA) ratio reveals that the business earned $13.90 before interest and income tax expenses on each $100 of assets. The ROA is compared with the annual interest rate on the company's borrowed money. In this example, the company's annual interest rate on its short-term and long-term debt is 7.5 percent. The business earned 13.9 percent on the money borrowed, as measured by the ROA. The difference or spread between the two rates is a favorable spread equal to 6.4 percentage points—which increases the earnings after interest for stockholders. This source of profit enhancement is called *financial leverage gain*. In contrast, if a company's ROA is less than its interest rate, it suffers a financial leverage loss.

Earnings per Share (EPS)

In contrast to the ratios discussed earlier in the chapter, the earnings per share (EPS) ratio is reported at the bottom of their income statements by public companies. You don't have to calculate it. Given its importance you should surely understand how it is calculated. Private companies do not report EPS. However, as a stockholder of a private company you may find it helpful to calculate its EPS.

The capital stock shares of 5,000 domestic business corporations are traded in public markets—the New York Stock Exchange, Nasdaq, and electronic stock exchanges. The day-to-day, even minute-by-minute market price changes of these shares receive a great deal of attention. More than any other single factor, the market value of capital stock shares depends on the past and forecast net income (earnings) of a business.

Suppose we tell you that the market price of a stock is $60, and ask you whether this value is too high or too low, or just about right. You could compare the market price with the stockholders' equity per share reported in the balance sheet—called the *book value per share*, which is about $29 in our example. (Recall that a company's total assets minus its total liabilities equal its stockholders' equity.) The book value method has a respectable history in securities analysis. Today, however, the book value approach plays second fiddle to the earnings-based approach. The starting point is to calculate *earnings (net income) per share*.

One of the most widely used ratios in investment analysis is *earnings per share* (EPS). The essential calculation of earnings per share is as follows for our company example:

$$\frac{\$2,642 \text{ Net Income Available for Common Stockholders}}{800,000 \text{ Shares of Common Stock Outstanding}} = \frac{\$3.30 \text{ Basic Earnings}}{\text{per Share}}$$

Note: To be technically accurate, the weighted average number of shares outstanding during the year should be used—based on the actual number of shares outstanding each month (or day) during the period.

First off, notice that the numerator (top number) in the EPS ratio is *net income available for common stockholders*, which equals bottom-line net income less any dividends paid to the preferred stockholders of the business. Many business corporations issue preferred stock that requires a fixed amount of dividends to be paid each year. The mandatory annual dividends to the preferred stockholders are deducted from net income to determine net income available for the common stockholders.

Second, please notice the word *basic* in front of *earnings per share*, which means that the actual number of common stock shares in the hands of stockholders is the denominator (bottom number) in the EPS calculation. Many business corporations have entered into contracts of one sort or another that require the company at some time in the future to issue additional stock shares at prices below the market value of the stock shares at that time. The shares under these contracts have not been actually issued yet but probably will be in the future.

For example, business corporations award managers *stock options* to buy common stock shares of the company at fixed prices (generally equal to the present market price or current value of the shares). If in the future the market value of the shares rises over the fixed option prices, the managers will exercise their rights and buy capital stock shares at a bargain price. With stock options, therefore, the number of stock shares is subject to inflation. When (and if) the additional shares are issued, EPS will suffer because net income will have to be spread over a larger number of stock shares. EPS will be diluted, or thinned down, because of the larger denominator in the EPS ratio.

Basic EPS does not recognize the additional shares that will be issued when stock options are exercised. Also, basic EPS does not take into account potential dilution effects of any convertible bonds and convertible preferred stock that have been issued by a business. These securities can be converted at the option of the security holders into common stock shares at predetermined prices.

To warn investors of the potential effects of stock options and convertible securities, a second EPS is reported by public corporations, called *diluted* EPS. This lower EPS takes into account the potential dilution effects caused by issuing additional common stock shares under stock option plans, convertible securities, and any other commitments a business has entered into that could require it to issue additional stock shares at predetermined prices in the future.

Basic EPS and diluted EPS (if applicable) must be reported in the income statements of publicly owned business corporations. This indicates the importance of EPS. In contrast, none of the other ratios discussed in this chapter have to be reported, although many public companies report selected ratios. For example, in its 2012 filing with the SEC Caterpillar included the times interest earned ratio.

Price/Earnings (P/E) Ratio

The market price of stock shares of a public business corporation is compared with its EPS and expressed in the *price/earnings (P/E) ratio* as follows:

$$\frac{\text{Current Market Price of Stock Shares}}{\text{Earnings per Share}} = \text{Price/Earnings Ratio}$$

Suppose a public company's stock shares are trading at $40 per share and its basic EPS for the most recent year (called the *trailing 12 months*) is $2. The company does not report a diluted EPS. Thus, its P/E ratio is 20. Like other ratios discussed in this chapter, the P/E ratio should be compared with industrywide and marketwide averages to judge whether it is acceptable, too high, or too low. At one time a P/E ratio of 8 was considered right. As we write this sentence P/E ratios in the range of 15 to 18 are considered acceptable and nothing to be alarmed about.

Now, here's a problem in calculating the P/E ratio for a public company: Should you use its *basic* EPS or its *diluted* EPS? If the business reports only basic EPS there is no problem. But when a public company reports both, which EPS should you use? Well, it is done both ways. Our advice is to check the legend in the stock market tables in the *Wall Street Journal* and the *New York Times* to find out which EPS the newspaper uses in reporting the P/E ratios for companies. Using diluted EPS is more conservative; that is, it gives a higher P/E ratio.

The market prices for stock shares of a private business are not available to the public at large. Private company shares are not usually actively traded and when they are traded the price per share is not made public. Nevertheless, stockholders in these businesses are interested in what their shares are worth. To estimate the value of stock shares a P/E multiple can be used. In the company example, its EPS is $3.30 for the most recent year (see Exhibit 18.1). Suppose you own some of the capital stock shares, and someone offers to buy your shares. You could establish an offer price at, say, 12 times basic EPS. This would be $39.60 per share. The potential buyer may not be willing to pay this price, or he or she might be willing to pay 15 or 18 times basic EPS.

Market Cap

Suppose the stock shares of a public company are currently trading at $65 per share, and the business has 10 million shares outstanding. The *market cap*, or total market value capitalization of the company, is $650 million ($65 market value per share ×10 million capital stock shares = $650 million). We'd bet you dollars to doughnuts that if you compared the market cap of most businesses with the shareholders' equity amounts reported in their latest balance sheets, the market caps would be considerably higher and perhaps much higher.

The book value (balance sheet value) of shareholders' equity is the historical record of the amounts invested in the business by the owners past plus its retained earnings accumulated over the years. Over time these amounts become more and more out of date. In contrast, the market cap is based on the current market value of the company's stock shares. If a business gets into financial straits, its market cap may drop below the book value of its owners' equity—at least for the time being. In rare cases a company's cash balance may be more than its market cap.

Final Comments

Many other ratios can be calculated from the data in financial statements. For example, the *asset turnover ratio* (annual sales revenue divided by total assets) and the *dividend yield* (annual cash dividends per share divided by market value per share) are two ratios you often see used in securities analysis. There's no end to the ratios that can be calculated.

The trick is to focus on those ratios that have the most interpretive value. It's not easy to figure out which ratios are the most important. Professional investors seem to use too many ratios rather than too few, in our opinion. On the other hand, you never know which ratio might provide a valuable clue to the future market value direction of a stock.

19

PROFIT ANALYSIS FOR BUSINESS MANAGERS

Unless you started reading this book in this chapter, you're aware that previous chapters focus on the *external financial statements* reported by businesses. As you probably know, accounting involves more than preparing a company's external financial statements, although this is certainly one of its most important functions.

Designing and operating accounting systems, complying with a myriad of tax laws, and preparing external financial reports are three bedrock accounting functions of every business. Also, the accounting staff in a business has another very important function—providing information to its managers for their decision-making, planning, and control. This fourth function of accounting is referred to as *management accounting* or *managerial accounting* (which we prefer).

Managerial Accounting

Managerial accounting is an *internal* function, which is carried out inside a business to help its managers make sound decisions, develop plans and budgets, and exercise control. In short, the purpose of managerial accounting is to help managers be good managers. Managerial accounting, more than anything else, should provide useful information needed by managers and help them make use of this information in the most effective manner.

The design of internal accounting reports to managers is dependent on the nature of the business and the organizational structure of the business. Suppose a business is divided into sales territories, for example. Accounting reports are needed for each sales territory. Each sales territory may be divided into major product lines. So, the accounting reports separate each product line in each territory. In short, management accounting should follow the organizational structure of a business and provide each manager with the information the manager needs.

External financial statements are designed for the outside, non-management investors and lenders of the business. The external accounting reports of a business do not contain all the financial information its managers need. Managers should understand their company's external financial statements like the backs of their hands, even though they are not accountants. And, they need additional accounting reports that provide more detailed information, much of which is confidential and is not released outside the confines of the business.

We could write a book on management control and the detailed information managers need for effective control. We could discuss in some detail the allocation of sales revenue and expenses to the *profit centers* and *cost centers* of a business. A profit center is a separate, identifiable source of sales revenue with its matching expenses. For an auto dealer, for instance, one profit center is its new car and truck sales; another is its used car and truck sales; and a third is its service and parts department. A cost center is an organizational unit that does not generate sales revenue, such as the accounting and building maintenance departments.

Before moving on, we should point out that this chapter is not a comprehensive survey of the field of managerial accounting—far from it! For instance, in this chapter we do not discuss budgeting, standard costs, management control reports, cost allocation methods, and other topics. Our more modest goal is to demonstrate how expenses should be classified, in order to make accounting information more useful for management decision-making analysis. We believe that business managers will find this chapter very instructive.

Beyond the Income Statement

To begin, see Exhibit 19.1. This is the exact duplicate of the company's externally reported income statement first seen in Exhibit 2.2. We repeat it here for ease of reference. There are no changes from earlier in the book.

Exhibit 19.1 shows a typical format for an *external* income statement. As you notice, this income statement reports highly condensed, summary-level information. As we have said several times before, this income statement is designed for reporting to the outside investors and lenders of a business entity. Is it adequate for the managers of the business? No, not by a long shot.

The first thought that probably comes to mind is that managers need a lot of detailed information for controlling the business than the condensed information in the external income statement. That's for sure! From the top line to the bottom line managers need more detailed and specific information. Take sales revenue, for instance. Managers, at least the ones responsible for sales, need information about how many units of each product were sold, which products didn't meet sales volume expectations and which exceeded forecasts. Also, managers should keep a close eye on product returns and postsale repairs and replacements of products.

For control purposes business managers need to keep track of a thousand and one details. Managers need to develop relevant performance benchmarks, and they should focus their time and energy on *control points*. For example, managers should keep a close watch on the total number of employees and sales revenue per employee. Productivity measures are very important for manufacturers. Retailers should measure inventory shrinkage in order to determine losses from customer shoplifting and employee theft.

In summary, accountants include a great deal more detailed information about sales revenue and expenses in internal income statements (profit reports) to managers. Managers need itemized information for controlling expenses. Therefore, the accountant

EXHIBIT 19.1—EXTERNAL INCOME STATEMENT FOR YEAR
Dollar Amounts in Thousands

Sales Revenue	$ 52,000
Cost of Goods Sold Expense	(33,800)
Gross Margin	$ 18,200
Selling, General, and Administrative Expenses	(12,480)
Depreciation Expense	(785)
Earnings before Interest and Income Tax	$ 4,935
Interest Expense	(545)
Earnings before Income Tax	$ 4,390
Income Tax Expense	(1,748)
Net Income	$ 2,642

provides supporting schedules listing hundreds or more specific expenses to managers. More than just detail, managers need to know how expenses behave relative to the two big profit drivers of every business—*sales prices* and *sales volume*.

To illustrate the importance of knowing how expenses behave, we put a question to you here. Which would be better for profit: a 5 percent sales price increase across the board, or a 5 percent sales volume increase on all products and services sold by the business? If you, the business manager, could have one but not the other, which would you choose—the sales price option or the sales volume option? One is clearly better, as we shall explain.

Classifying Operating Expenses

Refer to Exhibit 19.1 again please. Notice that cost of goods sold expense is deducted immediately after sales revenue, in order to determine the *gross margin* from sales (also called *gross profit*). Every business must earn an adequate gross margin to cover its other expenses. Earning a satisfactory bottom-line profit begins with earning an adequate gross margin on sales. Reporting cost of goods sold as a separate expense provides very important information for managers. No doubt about this. Managers, first and foremost, have to control their gross margins.

The next question concerns *operating expenses*, which in Exhibit 19.1 are lumped into one conglomerate account labeled *Selling, General, and Administrative Expenses*. Depreciation expense is reported separately in Exhibit 19.1, which is a special type of operating expense. (Operating expenses do not include interest and income tax expenses, which are reported separately in the income statement.)

The point we want to emphasize here is that business managers should understand how their expenses behave *relative to changes in sales revenue and sales volume*. Sales prices and sales volume are in a state of constant change for most businesses. Managers need to know how operating expenses change with changes in sales prices and sales volume. Unfortunately, this important point often gets overlooked in the hustle and bustle of the daily problems of running a business.

In our view, internal profit accounting reports to managers should classify operating expenses according to how they behave relative to changes in sales prices and sales volume. Sales prices and sales volume are the big two factors driving profit performance. In actual practice accountants generally do *not* classify expenses this way in their internal profit reports to managers. There are many reasons why they don't. For one thing, it would pile more work on top of all the other things accountants do in a business. Also, most managers probably don't ask for expense information to be classified this way. But we think managers are missing the boat on this. After reading this chapter, you'll have to be the judge on this issue.

Controlling specific operating expenses is one thing; analyzing operating expenses in decision-making is quite another. To emphasize this point, we recast the external income statement of our business example. See Exhibit 19.2, which we call the *Management Profit Report*. The company's operating expenses are classified according to how they behave relative to changes in sales prices and sales volume. It's an alternative to the standard external income statement.

In the management profit report (Exhibit 19.2), the company's operating expenses are classified into three types:

1. *Sales revenue expenses*—operating costs that depend on and vary with total sales revenue (the total dollar amount of sales). Sales commissions equal to a certain percent of sales and credit card discounts paid by a retailer to a credit card company are two examples.

EXHIBIT 19.2—MANAGEMENT PROFIT REPORT FOR YEAR

Dollar Amounts in Thousands

Sales Revenue	$ 52,000
Cost of Goods Sold Expense	(33,800)
Gross Margin	$ 18,200
Sales Revenue Expenses	(4,420)
Sales Volume Expenses	(3,120)
Profit Margin before Fixed Expenses	$ 10,660
Fixed Selling and Operating Expenses	(4,940)
Fixed Depreciation Expense	(785)
Earnings before Interest and Income Tax	$ 4,935
Interest Expense	(545)
Earnings before Income Tax	$ 4,390
Income Tax Expense	(1,748)
Net Income	$ 2,642

2. *Sales volume expenses*—operating costs that depend on and vary with the total sales volume, or quantities of products and services sold to customers. Packaging and transportation costs are two main examples.

3. *Fixed operating expenses*—costs that are relatively fixed in amount and cannot be changed over the short run. Employees on fixed salaries, building rent, equipment lease payments, and property taxes are examples of fixed operating costs. Depreciation is also a fixed expense because accountants allocate a fixed amount of depreciation to each period. Fixed costs can be reduced given enough time, but are more or less fixed over the short run.

The classification of operating expenses requires careful study to sort out which costs belong in each of the expense categories. Once its operating costs have been classified this way, the costs are tagged in the bookkeeping process so that the total for each type of operating expense is determined and included in internal profit reports to managers.

Comparing Changes in Sales Prices and Sales Volume

In the limited space of this chapter we can offer only a brief overview of how business managers can use a profit report like the one presented in Exhibit 19.2. Speaking broadly, business managers focus on *changes*. Every factor and variable that determines profit is subject to change; change is constant, as experienced business managers will verify. Managers have to deal with changes that affect the profit performance of their business.

For example, higher transportation costs next year may increase the company's sales volume driven expenses. Property taxes may go up, which will increase its fixed operating expenses. The sales manager may make a persuasive case that the advertising budget should be increased next year. Managers have to respond to all such changes; they don't get paid to sit on their hands and idly watch the changes happen.

Top-level managers have the responsibility of developing realistic plans to improve profit performance, which means making changes in the profit equation of the business. Which specific changes? This is the key question. Suppose the president of the company wants to develop a plan to improve bottom-line net income 10 percent next year. Exactly how would the manager accomplish this goal? The logical places to start are sales prices and sales volume.

Business managers need a crystal-clear understanding regarding what happens when sales prices increase (or decrease) and when sales volume increases (or decreases). In Exhibit 19.3 we compare the impacts of a 5 percent sales price increase scenario with a 5 percent sales volume increase scenario to help you appreciate the differences between changes in these two fundamental profit factors.

Before looking at Exhibit 19.3 you might first ask yourself which alternative you think is better. If you're a sales manager, you might favor the sales volume increase because the business would increase its market share at the higher sales volume. Market share is always an important factor to consider—you should never ignore this point. But, if you compare the two alternatives, you see that bumping the sales price 5 percent would be much better for profit.

In this comparison we stop at the earnings before interest and tax (EBIT) profit line. Generally, interest tends to follow sales revenue up and down, and income tax follows profit before income tax up and down—although we admit that these are very general comments.

Selling at 5 percent higher sales prices increases profit margin before fixed expenses 22.3 percent (see Exhibit 19.3), whereas selling 5 percent higher volume increases the profit margin before fixed expenses only 5 percent. Every variable expense goes up 5 percent with the 5 percent increase in sales volume. But only one expense goes up with the 5 percent sales price increase.

Then there are fixed selling and operating expenses and the fixed depreciation expense to consider. The higher sales prices shouldn't affect fixed costs. However, a higher sales volume would push up some fixed costs if the business is already running at

EXHIBIT 19.3—5% SALES PRICES VERSUS 5% SALES VOLUME INCREASE

Dollar Amounts in Thousands

	Original Example	5% Higher Sales Prices			5% Higher Sales Volume		
		New Scenario	Change Amount	Change Percent	New Scenario	Change Amount	Change Percent
Sales Revenue	$ 52,000	$ 54,600	$ 2,600	5.0%	$ 54,600	$ 2,600	5.0%
Cost of Goods Sold Expense	(33,800)	(33,800)			(35,490)	(1,690)	5.0%
Gross Margin	$ 18,200	$ 20,800	$ 2,600	14.3%	$ 19,110	$ 910	5.0%
Sales Revenue Sensitive Expenses	(4,420)	(4,641)	(221)	5.0%	(4,641)	(221)	5.0%
Sales Volume Sensitive Expenses	(3,120)	(3,120)			(3,276)	(156)	5.0%
Profit Margin before Fixed Expenses	$ 10,660	$ 13,039	$ 2,379	22.3%	$ 11,193	$ 533	5.0%
Fixed Selling and Operating Expenses	(4,940)	(4,940)			(4,940)		
Fixed Depreciation Expense	(785)	(785)			(785)		
EBIT	$ 4,935	$ 7,314	$ 2,379	48.2%	$ 5,468	$ 533	10.8%

full capacity and would have to add more space, equipment, and personnel to handle the higher sales volume. In Exhibit 19.3 we assume that the business could take on 5 percent more sales volume without having to increase any of its fixed costs.

It may be more realistic, though, to gain 5 percent more sales volume compared with pushing through a 5 percent sales price increase. Customers may balk at the higher sales prices. Setting sales prices certainly is one of the most perplexing decisions facing business managers. The price sensitivity of customers is seldom clear-cut. In any case, business managers should understand that a relatively small change in sales price could have a major impact on profit margin.

Breakeven Point

By definition the *breakeven point* is that mix of sales revenue and expenses that yields exactly a zero outcome—no profit and no loss. You can use the management profit report information (Exhibit 19.2) to determine the breakeven point at lower sales prices and lower sales volume. Exhibit 19.4 reveals that a 10.4 percent drop in sales prices would wipe out all the company's earnings before interest and income tax (EBIT). In contrast, sales volume would have to plunge 46.3 percent to take the business down to its EBIT breakeven point. (Using the Excel spreadsheet tool, we decreased sales price and sales volume to find the two breakeven points.)

Exhibit 19.4 makes clear that the business should be careful regarding lowering its sales prices. In particular, a 10 percent drop in sales prices would take the business very close to its breakeven point if volume stays the same. Its sales manager might suggest a cut in sales prices to boost sales volume. First, we'd recommend that you use the profit report (Exhibit 19.2) to crunch the numbers, and see whether profit would increase.

EXHIBIT 19.4—EBIT BREAKEVEN POINT FOR LOWER SALES PRICES AND LOWER SALES VOLUME
Dollar Amounts in Thousands

	Original Example	Sales Price Decrease				Sales Volume Decrease			
		Breakeven Scenario	Change			Breakeven Scenario	Change		
			Amount	Percent			Amount	Percent	
Sales Revenue	$ 52,000	$ 46,607	$ (5,393)	−10.4%		$ 27,929	$ (24,071)	−46.3%	
Cost of Goods Sold Expense	(33,800)	(33,800)				(18,154)	15,646	−46.3%	
Gross Margin	$ 18,200	$ 12,807	$ (5,393)	−29.6%		$ 9,775	$ (8,425)	−46.3%	
Sales Revenue Sensitive Expenses	(4,420)	(3,962)	458	−10.4%		(2,374)	2,046	−46.3%	
Sales Volume Sensitive Expenses	(3,120)	(3,120)				(1,676)	1,444	−46.3%	
Profit Margin before Fixed Expenses	$ 10,660	$ 5,725	$ (4,935)	−46.3%		$ 5,725	$ (4,935)	−46.3%	
Fixed Selling and Operating Expenses	(4,940)	(4,940)				(4,940)			
Fixed Depreciation Expense	(785)	(785)				(785)			
EBIT	$ 4,935	$ 0	$ (4,935)	−100.0%		$ 0	$ (4,935)	−100.0%	

Final Point

The format of the management profit report presented in Exhibit 19.3 can be used as a *template* or *model* for analyzing, budgeting, and planning profit. For instance, the business may plan for a 10 percent sales volume increase combined with 5 percent sales price increases across the board next year. You can easily make these changes and see what the profit (before interest and income tax expenses) would be if these changes hold true next year.

Part Five

TRUTHFULNESS

20

CHOOSING ACCOUNTING METHODS AND MASSAGING THE NUMBERS

Chapter Preamble

The accounting methods used to record the activities of a business and to prepare its financial statements should conform to authoritative financial accounting standards. These standards are always in a state of flux to one degree or another. The accountant should keep abreast of the latest changes in the standards. The shareowners and creditors who read the financial reports of a business are entitled to assume that its financial statements comply with current accounting standards, and that there are no serious violations of these standards.

The primary purpose of an audit of a financial report by an independent certified public accountant (CPA) is to ensure that proper accounting methods are used by the business and that it makes proper disclosure in its financial report. Chapter 21 discusses audits of financial reports by independent CPAs.

As you may have gathered from the chapter's title, the numbers reported in its financial statements depend on which *accounting methods* the business uses and whether the numbers have been massaged, or manipulated by the business. For that matter, the financial statements could be fraudulent and provide bogus numbers for sales revenue and expenses. Or a business may discover later that financial statements it has issued had serious errors. In this situation, the business issues a *restatement* of its original financial statements to set the record straight.

Financial statements have the appearance of accuracy and finality, don't they? In financial statements you see a lot of numbers that seem to be well organized and lined up in neat columns. But never lose sight of the fact that the numbers you see in financial statements depend on the accounting methods used to prepare the financial statements. And don't forget that if the recordkeeping process and accounting procedures of a business have errors (unintentional or deliberate), then its financial statements have errors—maybe very serious errors.

In this chapter we encourage you to develop a healthy skepticism when reading financial statements. First, you should understand that the profit performance of the business and the values of its assets and liabilities depend on which particular accounting methods are chosen by the business. Second, you should understand that a company's managers may take actions to affect the amounts of expenses and sales revenue for the year, in order to make profit come out closer to the number they want. Third, there's always a chance that the financial statements are fraudulent and seriously misleading. We don't want you to throw out the baby with the bathwater. But you should understand that some babies are given a bath in dirty water.

Let us make one thing clear: We believe that the large majority of businesses have reliable recordkeeping systems and use honest, good faith accounting methods. At the same time, the evidence is indisputable that many businesses do not exercise good faith in applying accounting methods and they deliberately prepare heavily biased or outright fraudulent financial statements. John's late father-in-law was a shrewd businessman who used to say, "There's a little bit of larceny in everyone's heart." We might say that there's a lot of larceny in the hearts of those businesses that put out misleading financial statements.

Choosing Accounting Methods

In choosing its accounting methods, a business should stay within the boundaries of authoritative accounting standards that apply to it. Don't think that the established standards put a business in a straitjacket regarding its accounting methods. Having accounting and reporting standards narrows down the range of choices but does not pin down a business to only one particular accounting method. In fact, for recording sales and many expenses a business can choose between alternative methods that are equally acceptable.

A business can adopt *conservative* accounting methods that delay the recording of profit, record lower values of certain assets, and record higher values of certain liabilities. Alternatively, a business can adopt *liberal* or *aggressive* accounting methods that have the reverse effects. Making decisions between liberal and conservative accounting methods is not a matter of choosing between good and bad accounting. Both conservative and liberal accounting methods are considered good accounting. Whether you vote Republican or Democratic doesn't mean you're a good or bad citizen.

Financial accounting would seem to be like measuring a person's weight on a scale that gives correct readings, wouldn't it? But, as a matter of fact, financial accounting standards permit a business to select which kind of scale to use—one that weighs light or one that weighs heavy.

This is not a textbook on accounting methods. All we can do here is give you a general idea of some areas in which a business can, quite legitimately, choose between alternative accounting methods. Here's a partial list of accounting methods that a business may have to choose between alternatives:

- The exact timing for recording sales as complete and final, particularly when customers can return products, when there are significant postsale expenses, and when sales prices are subject to later negotiation.

- When to record the expense of uncollectible accounts receivable from credit sales, and how to estimate the amount of these bad debts before they are actually written off at a future time.

- Whether to use first-in, first-out (FIFO), last-in, first-out (LIFO), or some other method for recording cost of goods sold expense and the cost value of inventory.

- Whether to use an accelerated (front-end loaded) depreciation method or the straight-line method, and whether to use short or longer (more realistic) useful life estimates.

- Whether to anticipate the likely loss in value of intangible assets or wait for clear evidence of the diminishment in value of intangible assets before recording the expense.

- Whether to immediately recognize future warranty and guarantee costs for products sold or wait until the work is done in later periods.

◆ Whether to use low-end or high-end estimates for key variables that determine the cost of an employee-defined benefit retirement plan and a postretirement health/medical benefit plan.

This list is just a sampling of the decisions a business has to make for recording sales revenue and expenses. The net income for the period depends on the accounting methods selected by the business. In summary, a business has many accounting choices. According to financial reporting standards it must disclose its significant accounting methods in the footnotes to its financial statements. (Chapter 17 discusses footnotes.)

Most business managers probably welcome having a choice of accounting methods. In fact, they might prefer to have a broader range of choices for their accounting methods and for their financial report disclosures. The evolution of accounting standards over the years has been in the direction of narrowing the range of approved accounting methods and expanding financial reporting disclosure requirements.

Note: A business does not have to disclose the difference it would have made in its net income and in its asset and liability values if it had used alternative accounting methods. A business doesn't have to go to the trouble of recomputing its sales revenue and all its expenses as if alternative accounting methods had been used instead of the accounting methods it actually uses. For example, a business does *not* say anything such as the following in its financial report:

> In the footnotes to the financial statements we explain that we use conservative accounting methods. If, instead, we had used liberal accounting methods, net income for the year just ended would have been $50 million higher, and assets and liabilities would have been significantly different than the amounts reported in the year-end balance sheet.

Finally, keep in mind that the choice of accounting methods does not affect cash flows during the year. The statement of cash flows (see Chapters 14 and 15) is the same regardless of which accounting methods are used. The statement of cash flows reports actual cash flows that occurred during the period. (However, a business may use a questionable technique called *window dressing* to improve its ending cash balance, which we discuss later in the chapter.)

Massaging the Numbers

During the year, business managers get regular profit reports from their accounting department. Toward the end of the year, and perhaps sooner, they should have a pretty good idea of the profit number that will be reported in the company's annual income statement. The projected profit may be significantly lower than they had forecast for the year (or much higher, for that matter). Broadly speaking, business managers have two courses of action in such a situation.

The managers could conduct business as usual. This means that they don't do anything special to deliberately affect the numbers that will be recorded for sales revenue and expenses in the year. (This does not preclude reducing costs where they can.) Or the managers could take action to cause net income for the year to come closer to what they want it to be. There are various steps managers can take to make net income "behave," as it were.

In short, managers can do certain things for the main purpose of reducing or increasing expenses for the year (and sales revenue also). These management actions are generally called *massaging the numbers*. Managers put their thumbs on the scale, as it were, which has the effect of boosting or dampening the recorded profit for the year. Massaging the numbers raises ethical and moral questions that, unfortunately, do not have easy and clear-cut answers.

Let us make clear the distinction between massaging the numbers and *cooking the books*. The latter term refers to *accounting fraud*. Fraud goes way beyond massaging the numbers. Fraud involves falsifying sales revenue and expense amounts. Massaging the numbers refers to situations in which a business has recorded legitimate sales revenue and expenses, but managers take action to nudge the numbers up or down for the year. The best description of massaging the numbers we've heard was from John's late father-in-law, a successful business owner/manager in his day. He said it was like "fluffing the pillows." We've always liked that characterization.

One can argue that massaging the numbers is not any worse than telling white lies, or embellishing the truth for the sake of a good story. Some say that massaging the numbers is like putting cosmetics on the financial face of the business (like putting lipstick on a pig in some cases, we would say).

Most accountants are uncomfortable with it, but they understand that massaging the numbers is tolerated in the worlds of business and finance. (A Catholic might look on massaging the numbers as a venial sin, but cooking the books would be a mortal sin.) Accountants would prefer that business managers not do it, but they go along with massaging the accounting numbers. You hardly ever hear of an accountant that blew the whistle on a business for massaging its numbers. You could argue that the reason for this silence is that the company's accountant is a member of its management team. CPA auditors also tolerate some degree of massaging the numbers. (More on this in Chapter 21.)

One reason that managers massage their accounting numbers is to *smooth reported profit* year to year. Managers think that left on its own the accounting system generates net income numbers that behave too erratically, and that are too jerky year to year. They justify massaging the numbers on the grounds that they should "sand off the rough edges" of profit year to year. They argue that investors are better off because they don't overreact to year-to-year perturbations in reported net income because the business reports a flatter trend line of earnings.

Well, such reasoning for massaging the numbers is difficult to judge. When a business has manipulated its accounting numbers for the year, it does not disclose what net income would have been without intervention by management. In any case, investors and creditors should realize that there's a good chance that the accounting numbers in the financial statements they are reading have been manipulated (massaged) to one degree or another.

Managers can massage the numbers in a variety of ways. For example, most businesses have *discretionary expenses*, which are those that depend heavily on the judgment of managers regarding how much to spend and when to make the expenditures. Consider repair and maintenance costs, for instance. Until the work is actually done, no expense is recorded. A manager can simply move back (or move up) the work orders for these expenditures. The building isn't painted this year, though it was scheduled to be. Or tires on delivery trucks are not replaced until next year. Using such tactics, a manager controls the amounts of some expenses that are recorded in the year.

Most businesses have many discretionary expenses. Two other discretionary expenses come to mind—employee training and development costs, and advertising expenditures. The manager in charge can delay sending employees on their normal schedule of training courses. An advertising campaign could be delayed until next year. The subsequent impacts of these actions on employee productivity and sales are difficult to assess.

Another way in which managers can massage the accounting numbers involves the *end-of-year adjusting entries* that are recorded to bring certain expenses up to their full and complete balances for the year. Many of these year-end adjusting entries require estimates: the amount of accounts receivable that may not be collected in the future, the costs of future warranty work on products sold to customers, the rate of return that will be earned on the funds in the defined benefit employee retirement plan sponsored by the business, the decline in value of its intangible assets, and so on. Managers can lay a heavy hand on these estimates, thereby controlling the amount of expenses recorded in the year.

Managers can take certain actions to boost the amount of sales revenue recorded in the year. Sales can be accelerated, for example, by shipping more products to the company's captive dealers, even though they didn't order the products. This is called stuffing the channels of distribution. The business is taking away sales from next year to put the sales on the books this year. There are many other ways a business can give its sales for the year an artificial boost.

So far we have discussed massaging the numbers from the point of view of manipulating the amount of profit (net income) reported for the year. There is also a type of massaging the numbers that does not affect profit. Instead, the purpose is to make the short-term solvency and liquidity of the business look better than it really was at the end of the year. One practice is called *window dressing*.

Here's a common example of window dressing. A business holds open its books (its accounting records) for a few days after the end of its accounting year. The purpose is to record additional cash collections of accounts receivable. The cash collections are not actually received and in the hands of the company until the first few days in January 2014, for example, but the cash inflows are recorded as if they were collected December

31, 2013. The result is that its cash balance is higher and its accounts receivable is lower, which makes the company look more liquid (a larger cash balance). When we were in public accounting, we had clients who did this regularly. We suspect the same is true today.

Again, we should make clear that cooking the books goes beyond massaging the numbers. Cooking the books refers to recording sales revenue when in fact no sales were made, and not recording actual expenses or losses during the period. In short, cooking the books involves falsification of the accounting records. If massaging the numbers is carried too far, it can end up being equivalent to cooking the books (i.e., accounting fraud). In other words, massaging the numbers is a slippery slope that can lead to accounting fraud.

Business Managers and Their Accounting Methods

The chief executive officer (CEO) of a business has the responsibility that the company's financial statements are fairly presented. This means that the accounting methods used to measure the company's profit comply with the established accounting standards that apply to the business. If its accounting methods are outside these limits, the company could stand accused of issuing false and misleading financial statements. The CEO would be liable for damages suffered by the company's creditors and stockholders who relied on its misleading financial statements. If for no other reason than this, the CEO should pay close attention to the choices of accounting methods used to prepare the company's financial statements.

Ideally, the chief executive of the business and its other top-level managers should decide which accounting methods and policies are best for the company. The top-level managers should seek the advice of the company's chief financial officer and controller (chief accountant). They have to decide between conservative (cautious) versus liberal (aggressive) profit-accounting methods, which means whether to record profit later (cautious) or sooner (aggressive). The sooner sales revenue is recorded, the earlier profit is reported; and the later expenses are recorded, the earlier profit is reported.

If a business wants to report profit as soon as possible, the CEO should instruct the accountants to choose those accounting methods that accelerate sales revenue and delay expenses. In contrast, if the business wants to be conservative, it should order its accountants to use those accounting methods that delay the recording of sales revenue and accelerate the recording of expenses, so that profit is reported as late as possible. The accounting methods selected for cost of goods sold expense and depreciation expense are two key choices for businesses that sell products and invest heavily in long-term operating (fixed) assets.

Business managers may prefer to avoid getting involved in choosing accounting methods. We think this is a mistake. Somebody has to choose the accounting methods—if not its managers, then by default probably the company's controller. The controller, being the chief accounting officer of the company, should work hand in glove with the CEO and the other top-level managers to make sure that the accounting methods used by the business are not working at cross-purposes with the goals, objectives, strategies, and plans of the organization.

Consistency of Accounting Methods

Once a business chooses which accounting methods to use, the business sticks with these methods. A company does not flip-flop between accounting methods year to year. For one thing the Internal Revenue Service takes a dim view of switching accounting methods one year to the next. Furthermore, changing accounting methods causes a lot of disclosure problems in a business's financial statements and footnotes. Changes in accounting methods may be needed in unusual circumstances, but the large majority of businesses don't switch their accounting methods except on rare occasions.

In short, consistency of accounting methods is the norm. Investors and lenders demand consistency of accounting methods year to year. Inconsistency would cause all sorts of problems in their year-to-year comparative analysis of a company's financial statements. It's tough enough as it is to analyze financial statements. Inconsistency of accounting methods would add another layer of difficulty. Financial accounting standards do not prohibit changing accounting methods. However, a business should change methods only if there is sufficient reason to do so.

Quality of Earnings

You see the phrase *quality of earnings* in the business and financial press. Reported net income is put to a quality test, or litmus test as it were. The term does not have a uniform definition, but most persons who use this term refer to the integrity and trustworthiness of the accounting methods used by a business.

Conservative accounting methods are generally viewed as high quality. Stock analysts and professional investment managers view aggressive accounting methods with more caution. They like to see some margin for safety or some cushion for a rainy day in a company's accounting numbers. They know that many estimates and choices have to be made in financial accounting, and they would just as soon a business err on the low side in reporting profit rather than the high side.

Professional investors and investment managers are especially alert for accounting methods that appear to record revenue (or other sources of income) too early, or that fail to record losses or expenses that should be recognized. Even though the financial statements are audited, investment professionals go over them with a fine-tooth comb to get a better feel for how trustworthy are the reported earnings of a business.

A basic principle of investing in stocks is to diversify your portfolio, so that investment risks are not too concentrated in just one stock or only a few stock holdings. One risk is that a company's financial report may be misleading, based on suspect accounting methods, or even be fraudulent. Therefore, diversifying your stock holdings offers some protection against the risk of misleading and fraudulent financial reports.

21

AUDITS OF FINANCIAL REPORTS

A business may hire an independent CPA to audit its financial report. Many people think an audit is done for the purpose of discovering wrongdoing or ferreting out dishonest and illegal behavior. A CPA is duty bound to maintain a mental attitude of professional skepticism in doing an audit. In carrying out audit procedures the CPA may discover embezzlement or theft by employees, or uncover accounting fraud orchestrated by high-level managers. These are by-products or side effects of an audit. The main purpose of an audit by a CPA is something else.

The CPA auditor examines accounting records and gathers other evidence in order to render an opinion on the financial report of the business. Based on the audit the CPA attests, or "swears" to the *fairness* of the financial statements and disclosures in the financial report of the business. Fairness means, primarily, that the company's accounting methods and disclosures are in accordance with established accounting and financial reporting standards that apply to the entity. In short, the CPA auditor states whether or not the business is playing fairly according to the rules in its financial report.

Why Audits?

Suppose you have invested a fair amount of money in a privately owned business. You are not involved in managing the company; you're an absentee owner—a passive investor. Being a stockholder, you receive the company's financial reports. You read the financial statements and footnotes to keep informed about how the company is doing, and whether there might be any storm clouds on the horizon.

Let us ask you a question: How do you know whether the company's financial statements provide adequate disclosure and whether the business uses proper accounting methods to measure its profit? Do you just presume this? Are you sure you can trust the company's financial reports?

Or suppose you are a bank loan officer. A business includes its latest financial statements in its loan application package. Does the business use correct accounting methods to prepare its financial statements? Have the financial statements been tweaked for purposes of securing the loan, to make them look better than they really are? It's not unheard of, you know. (See Chapter 20 on massaging the numbers in financial statements.)

Or suppose you're a mutual fund investment manager in charge of a large portfolio of stocks traded on the New York Stock Exchange and Nasdaq. Market values of stock shares depend on the net income and earnings per share amounts reported by companies in their financial reports. How do you know that their profit numbers are reliable?

Financial statements can be seriously misleading for two basic reasons, one type being innocent in nature and the other type not so innocent:

1. *Honest mistakes and incompetency:* A company may not have adequate internal accounting controls. Accounting errors can become imbedded in its accounting records, and the business fails to detect and correct the errors. Or, its chief accountant may not understand current accounting and financial reporting requirements and standards.

2. *Deliberate dishonesty:* The top-level managers of a business may intentionally distort the company's profit performance and financial statements, or withhold vital information that should be disclosed in the financial report. This is called financial reporting fraud or accounting fraud. More popularly, it's called *cooking the books*.

One way to protect against the risks of errors and fraud is to conduct an *audit* of the accounting system of the business by an independent expert accountant, to ascertain whether its financial statements are free of errors and adhere to appropriate accounting and financial reporting standards. The audit provides reassurance that the company's financial report is reliable and follows the rules. Audits of financial reports are done by independent *certified public accountants*, the profession we turn to next.

Certified Public Accountant (CPA)

A person needs to do three things to become a certified public accountant (CPA). He or she must earn a college degree with a major in accounting with a fairly heavy load of accounting and auditing courses. The American Institute of Certified Public Accountants (AICPA) has encouraged all states to enact laws requiring five years of education. Most but not quite all states have passed such laws.

Second, a person must pass the national CPA exam, which is a rigorous exam testing knowledge in accounting, income tax, auditing, and business law. Third, a person must satisfy the experience requirement of the state in which he or she lives. State laws and regulations differ regarding the time and nature of public accounting experience that a person must have; one year is generally the minimum.

After the three requirements are completed—education, exam, and experience—the person receives a license by his or her state of residence to practice as a CPA. No one else may hold him- or herself out to the public as a CPA. Most states (perhaps all, but we haven't checked this out) require 30 or 40 hours of continuing education each year to renew a person's CPA license. Every state has a Board of Accountancy that regulates the practice of public accounting and has the power to revoke or suspend the licenses of individuals who violate the laws, regulations, and ethics governing CPAs.

CPAs do more than just audit financial reports. They offer an ever-widening range of services to the public—income tax compliance and planning, personal financial consulting, business valuation, computer systems and information technology, production control and efficiency, forensic functions, and other fields of specialization. (*Note:* CPA firms that audit the financial reports of *public* companies are under tight restrictions regarding which particular nonaudit services they can provide to their audit clients.)

The CPA license is widely recognized and highly respected as a professional credential. The professional status of CPAs rests on their expertise and experience, and their independence from their clients. The word *certified* in their title refers to their expertise and experience. The term *public* refers to their independence. In doing audits of financial statements, the independence of the CPA is absolutely essential. To be independent, a CPA must be in public practice and not be an employee of any organization (other than the CPA firm itself).

Public accounting experience is a good stepping-stone to other career opportunities. Many persons start in public accounting and end up as the controller (chief accountant), financial vice president, or chief financial officer (CFO) of an organization. Some CPAs become presidents and chief executive officers (CEOs) of business organizations. Some CPAs go into politics (a few have become state governors). Persons who have left public accounting are still referred to as CPAs even though they are not in public practice any longer. This is like a person with an MD degree who leaves the practice of medicine but is still called *doctor*.

Are Audits Required?

Corporations whose debt and stock securities are traded publicly are required by federal securities laws to have their annual financial reports audited by an independent CPA firm. According to a recent survey there are about 5,000 companies listed on major securities exchanges in the United States (which is down considerably from just a few years ago). The number of private businesses, in the usual sense of the word *business*, is more difficult to pin down. In the United States there are more than 9 million for-profit business corporations, partnerships, and limited liability companies, as well as millions of sole proprietorships (one-owner business ventures). Private businesses are not covered by federal securities laws, but are subject to such state laws as apply to them. Although they are not *legally required* to have audits, many private business entities have their annual financial reports audited by a CPA firm.

Lawyers should be consulted regarding state corporation and securities laws; an audit may be required in certain situations. A private business may sign a contract or agree informally to have its annual financial reports audited by an independent CPA as a condition of borrowing money or when issuing capital stock to new investors in the business.

Public corporations have no choice; they are legally required to have audits of their annual financial reports by an independent CPA firm. But, if not required, should a business hire a CPA firm to audit its annual financial report? What's the payoff? Basically, an audit adds *credibility* to the financial report of a business.

Audited financial reports have a higher "believability index" than unaudited statements.

Audits by CPAs provide protection against misleading financial statements. CPA auditors are expert accounting detectives, and they thoroughly understand accounting and financial reporting standards. Being independent of a business, the CPA auditor should not tolerate a misleading financial report.

Audits don't come cheap. CPAs are professionals who command high fees. A business cannot ask for an "once-over lightly" audit at a cut rate. An audit is an audit. CPA auditors of private businesses are bound by *generally accepted auditing standards* (GAAS), and the auditors of public companies have to follow the regulations of the federal agency created by the Sarbanes-Oxley Act of 2002. Violations of auditing standards and regulations can result in lawsuits against the CPA, sanctions by the federal regulatory agency, and damage to the CPA's professional reputation.

An audit takes a lot of time because the CPA has to examine a great deal of evidence and make many tests of the accounting records of the business before being able to express an opinion on the company's financial statements. The time it takes to complete an audit causes the relatively high cost of the audit. A business, assuming an audit is not legally required, has to ask whether the gain in credibility of its financial report is worth the cost of the audit.

A bank may insist on an audit as a condition of making a loan to a business. The outside (nonmanagement) stockholders of a business may insist on annual audits to protect their investments in the business. In these situations, the audit fee can be viewed as a cost of using external capital. In many situations, however, outside investors and creditors do not insist on audits. Even so, a business may choose to have an audit as a checkup on its accounting system. Or a business may decide it needs to have a forensic check—an independent examination focusing on whether the business is vulnerable to fraud and embezzlement schemes.

An annual audit by a CPA is like an individual having a general physical exam once a year. The physician performs standard tests and evaluates your overall condition, and at the same time should be alert for any trouble signs out of the ordinary. Unless there is some reason to look for cancer or heart problems, the doctor does not do extensive examinations for these problems. For instance, the doctor doesn't order an X-ray unless he or she suspects a problem that requires this additional procedure.

The auditor does not examine every transaction of a business during the year and does not examine every item making up the total balance of specific assets and liabilities. In a word, auditors rely a great deal on *sampling*. CPA auditors, therefore, pay particular attention to the *internal controls* of the company that are designed to deter and detect errors and irregularities. CPA auditors are required to carry out *risk assessment procedures*, to identify the likely areas of errors and irregularities and to concentrate their audit procedures in the high-risk areas.

CPA auditors are required to plan their audit procedures to search for possible accounting fraud and to identify weak internal controls that would allow such fraud to go undetected. Nevertheless, the main purpose of an audit is to express an opinion on the fairness of financial statements (including footnotes), and whether the financial statements adhere to appropriate accounting and financial reporting standards.

Fraud would undermine the integrity of the financial statements, so the CPA auditor has to be on the lookout for fraud of all types (as well as for accounting errors). But the CPA says nothing at all about fraud in the audit report. There is no statement such as "We looked for fraud but didn't find any." We discuss what the CPA auditor does say next.

Clean Audit Opinion

First of all, let's be clear on one point. We are talking specifically about *audits of business financial reports by a CPA*. There are many other kinds of audits, such as an audit of your income tax return by the Internal Revenue Service (IRS), audits of federally supported programs by the Government Accountability Office (GAO), audits by the internal auditors of an organization, and so on. The following discussion concerns audits by CPAs of financial reports prepared by businesses that are released to the outside world—primarily to their lenders, shareholders, and others who have a right to receive a copy of the financial report.

Financial report readers are not too concerned about how an audit is done, nor should they be. The bottom line to them is the opinion of the CPA auditor. They should read the opinion carefully, although there is evidence that most don't or at best just give it a quick glance. Evidently many financial report readers simply assume that having the financial report audited is, by itself, an adequate safeguard. They assume that the CPA would not be associated with a financial report that is incorrect or misleading.

Many financial report readers seem to think that if the CPA firm gives an opinion and thereby is associated with a financial report, then the financial statements and footnotes must be okay and are not wrong in any significant respect. Doesn't the CPA's opinion constitute a stamp of approval? No, not necessarily!

The best audit opinion is termed an *unqualified opinion*, or more popularly is called a *clean* opinion. Basically this unqualified, or clean, opinion states that the CPA has no significant disagreements with the financial statements and disclosures of the company. Putting it differently, the CPA *attests* that the financial statements have been prepared according to appropriate accounting and financial reporting standards and that the footnotes plus other information in the financial report provide adequate disclosure. (These standards leave management a range of choices of accounting methods, which we discuss in Chapter 20.)

The standard language for a clean, or unqualified opinion for a business named the XYZ Company, Inc. that uses U.S. accounting standards goes like the following:

> In our opinion, the financial statements referred to above present fairly, in all material respects, the financial position of XYZ Company, Inc. as of December 31, 2014, and the results of its operations and its cash flows for the year then ended in accordance with U.S. generally accepted accounting principles.

This is called the *opinion paragraph*. The auditor's report also contains other parts including an opening paragraph, a reminder about management's responsibility for the financial statements, and a fairly lengthy discussion about the auditor's responsibility (and limits of responsibility) in doing the audit. We spare you reading these other parts of the auditor's report. The bottom line of an auditor's report is the opinion paragraph. The most important words are *present fairly*. What exactly do these two words mean?

In a clean opinion, the CPA auditor says, in effect, "we don't disagree with the financial report." The CPA, if he or she were the controller of the business, might have prepared the financial statements differently and might have written the footnotes differently. In fact, the CPA auditor might prefer that different accounting methods had been used. What the CPA expresses in a clean opinion is that the company's financial statements and disclosures do not in any material manner violate established accounting and financial reporting standards.

The standard version of the CPA auditor's report runs more than 200 words of fairly technical jargon, and in our opinion demands a lot from the reader. Even if you're in a hurry, or just don't want to struggle though the whole auditor's report be sure to read the auditor's opinion.

Do Auditors Discover Accounting Fraud?

In Chapter 20 we distinguish between *massaging the numbers* and *accounting fraud*. Massaging the numbers involves nudging accounting numbers one way or the other. Business managers take actions to control the amounts of sales revenue and expenses recorded in the period, in order to smooth profit year to year or to give profit a temporary boost up (or a push down). Such accounting tactics are in a gray area of accounting ethics. CPA auditors certainly don't like to discover these management machinations regarding the accounting numbers. However, manipulating the accounting numbers is tolerated in the business world—as long as it doesn't go too far so as to cause seriously misleading financial statements.

Massaging the numbers can be likened to a misdemeanor. In this vein, accounting fraud is a felony. Cooking the books goes way beyond nudging the numbers up or down a little. Accounting fraud involves falsification or fabrication of sales revenue and expenses, and reporting assets that don't exist or not reporting liabilities that do exist. In short, accounting fraud creates financial statements that are deliberately misleading—and seriously so.

Do CPA auditors always discover accounting fraud? The short answer is: not necessarily. CPA auditors *may* discover accounting fraud. However, if the managers who commit fraud cleverly conceal the fraud and if their schemes are well thought out, accounting fraud can go undiscovered for years. There are many examples of companies carrying on fraud for 5, 10, or more years. In many cases the fraud collapses of its own weight or someone blows the whistle. But, having an audit by an independent CPA certainly increases the chances of uncovering accounting fraud, even though the audit does not guarantee that fraud will be uncovered in every instance.

What it comes down to, in our view, is that the cost of an audit has to be kept under control. The audit cost has to be reasonable relative to the benefits of the audit. Given the cost constraint on an audit, the CPA cannot search and test for every conceivable fraud that could be going on in the business. The CPA auditor should evaluate the controls established by the business to guard against financial reporting fraud. If the auditor discovers weaknesses in these controls, the auditor should investigate the vulnerable areas and work closely with the company's audit committee to remedy the weaknesses.

At the end of the day, there's always some risk that the CPA auditor may not discover accounting fraud—especially if the top-level managers of the business instigate and orchestrate the fraud. The cost of making all audits absolutely fail-safe would be prohibitive. In the grand scheme of things, a few audit failures are tolerated in order to keep the overall cost of audits within reason. In moments of deep cynicism, it has occurred to us that perhaps the real reason for audits is to provide business lenders and investors someone else to sue when they suffer losses and there is evidence that the company's financial report was seriously misleading or fraudulent.

Reading an Auditor's Report

The majority of financial report readers, in our opinion, simply want to know whether the CPA has any objection to the financial statements and footnotes prepared by management. They don't care that much about the specific wording used in the CPA auditor's report. They want to know one main thing: Does the CPA auditor give his or her blessing to management's financial report? If not, they want the CPA auditor to make clear his or her objections to the financial report.

Financial report users should read the CPA auditor's report to see first, whether the auditor gives a clean opinion, and second, whether the auditor provides any additional information that might constitute something less than a clean opinion. The standard audit report is expanded or modified in the following situations:

- The CPA auditor wants to emphasize one or more points, such as related-party transactions reported in the financial statements, significant events during the year, or unusual uncertainties facing the business.

- The company has changed its accounting methods between the most recent year and previous years, which causes inconsistencies with the originally issued financial reports of the business.

- There is substantial doubt about the entity's ability to continue as a going concern, because of financial difficulties in meeting the due dates for payment of its liabilities, or because of other large liabilities it is not able to pay.

Such additional information in the audit report does not constitute a qualification on the company's financial report; it just provides more information.

In contrast, the CPA auditor may take exception to an accounting method used by the company, or to the lack of disclosure for some item that the CPA thinks is necessary for adequate disclosure. In this situation, the CPA renders a *qualified opinion* that includes the key words *except for* in the opinion paragraph. The grounds for the qualification (what the auditor takes exception to) are explained in the auditor's report. To give a qualified opinion, the CPA auditor must be satisfied that, taken as a whole, the financial statements and footnotes are not misleading.

A qualified opinion may be due to a limitation on the scope of the CPA's examination (collection of evidence). The CPA is not able to gather sufficient evidence for one or more accounts in the financial statements, and therefore has to qualify or restrict his or her opinion with regard to these items.

How serious a matter is a qualified opinion? The auditor points out a flaw in the company's financial report, but not a fatal flaw. A qualified audit opinion is a yellow flag, not a red flag. Keep one thing in mind: The CPA auditor must judge that the overall fairness of the financial report is satisfactory, even though there are one or more deviations from established accounting and disclosure standards. If the auditor is of the opinion that the deviations are so serious as to make the financial statements misleading, then the CPA must issue an *adverse opinion*. You hardly ever see an adverse opinion. No business wants to put out misleading financial statements and have the CPA auditor say so for everyone to see!

A CPA auditor may have to *disclaim an opinion* due to limitations on the scope of the audit or due to very unusual uncertainties facing the business. In some situations a CPA may have very serious disagreements with the client that cannot be resolved to the auditor's satisfaction. The CPA may withdraw from the engagement (i.e., walk off the audit). This is not very common, but it happens every now and then. In these situations the CPA has to notify top management, the board of directors of the company, and its audit committee, and make clear the nature of the disagreements and why the CPA is withdrawing from the audit.

The CPA does not act as a whistle-blower beyond the inner confines of the company. For public companies, the CPA has to inform the SEC and its Public Company Accounting Oversight Board that the firm has withdrawn from the audit engagement and whether there were any unresolved disagreements between the CPA and the company. Also, the CPA auditor should work closely with the audit committee of a public company, and is duty-bound to communicate to the committee issues that come up in the course of the audit.

Post-SOX

Congress passed the Sarbanes-Oxley Act of 2002 (SOX) in response to many well-publicized audit failures, culminating in the infamous Enron fiasco. This important piece of federal legislation is designed to improve the quality of audits and the independence of CPA auditors. Congress was upset with the fact that auditors failed to discover enormous accounting frauds that happened under their very noses. Congress was in no mood to hear any more excuses and promises from the auditing profession.

The act created a new federal agency called the *Public Company Accounting Oversight Board* (PCAOB), which is a branch of the Securities and Exchange Commission (SEC). The PCAOB has enormous power over the CPA firms that audit public companies. It might have been better to call the board the "Public Company *Auditing* Oversight Board." The PCAOB is given broad powers and has the dominant role in regulating the auditing of public companies.

The Sarbanes-Oxley Act also imposed financial reporting duties on corporate management. The CEO has to certify that his or her company's financial report is presented fairly and is in full compliance with all relevant accounting and financial reporting standards. Also, management is required to state its opinion on the internal controls of the business in the annual financial reports.

The CPA auditing profession is presently split into two basic segments: audits of *public* companies and audits of *private* companies. The Auditing Standards Board of the AICPA issues authoritative auditing pronouncements that govern audits of private companies. The PCAOB controls the rules for auditing public companies, although areas in which the agency has not taken action are still governed by the standards of the AICPA's Auditing Standards Board.

22

BASIC QUESTIONS, BASIC ANSWERS

Some years ago a women's investment club invited John to their monthly meeting to explain financial statements. It was a lot of fun. These women were a savvy group of investors who pooled their monthly contributions and invested mainly in common stocks traded on the major securities exchanges.

These women investors asked thoughtful questions. We share these with you in this chapter, and answer a couple of other questions that are important for anyone who invests in stock and debt securities issued by public corporations, or who has an investment in a private business. Other financial statement readers will also find this chapter helpful.

Business investors and lenders should know the answers to certain questions concerning financial statements. We answer these questions from the viewpoint of a typical individual investor, not an institutional investor or a professional investment manager. John's retirement fund (TIAA-CREF) manages about $400 billion of investments. We assume its portfolio managers know the answers to these questions. They'd better!

When You Sell a Stock Does the Company Get Your Money?

One point caught John quite by surprise, and it's an important one to understand. At that time the women were thinking of buying common stock shares of General Electric (GE). Two members presented their research on the company with the recommendation to buy the stock at the going market price. The discussion caused John to suspect that several of the members thought their money would go to GE. John pointed out that the money would go to the seller of the stock shares, not to GE.

They were not entirely clear on the difference between the *primary* capital market (the original issue of securities by corporations for money that flows directly into their coffers), and the *secondary* securities trading market (in which people sell securities they already own to other investors, with no money going to the companies that originally issued the securities). John compared this with the purchase of a new car in which money goes to General Motors, Ford, or Honda (passing through the dealer) versus the purchase of a used car in which the money goes to the previous owner.

John cleared up that point, although he thinks they were disappointed that GE would not get their money. Once John pointed out the distinction between the two capital markets, they realized that whereas they were of the opinion that the going market value was a good price to buy at, the person on the other side of the trade must think it was a good price to sell at.

Are Financial Reports Reliable and Trustworthy?

Yes, the large majority of financial reports by *public* companies are presented fairly according to established standards, which are called *generally accepted accounting principles* (GAAP) in the United States and *international financial reporting standards* (IFRS) outside the United States. If not, the company's CPA auditor calls deviations or shortcomings to your attention. So, be sure to read the CPA auditor's report. The U.S. and international accounting and financial reporting standards have not yet (2013) been completely merged into one set of converged standards—if they ever will be. How, and when this "harmonization" process will end up is hard to predict.

The financial reports of *private* companies that are audited by CPAs are as generally reliable as those of public companies. (At least this has been our experience.) However, *unaudited* financial reports of private companies are more at risk of violating one or more accounting and financial reporting standards. For example, we have seen private company annual financial reports that did not include a statement of cash flows, even though this financial statement was required at the time. Much depends on the competence of the chief accountant of the business. When reading unaudited financial statements of smaller private companies, you should be more on guard particularly if there is no statement of cash flows in the annual financial report.

You should realize that accounting and financial reporting standards are not static. The rule-making authorities constantly monitor financial reporting practices and identify emerging problem areas. They make changes when needed, especially to keep abreast of changes in business and financial practices, as well as developments in the broader political, legal, and economic environments in which businesses live and operate.

Nevertheless, Are Some Financial Statements Misleading and Fraudulent?

Yes, unfortunately. The *Wall Street Journal* and the *New York Times* carry stories of accounting fraud instigated by high-level managers in businesses. These financial report shenanigans are done in various ways. Sales revenue can be overstated. Expenses and losses can be understated or not recorded at all. Net income can be inflated in order to prop up the market price of the stock shares. Or, a business may not disclose serious problems in its financial condition. In committing accounting fraud, the business lies to its lenders and shareowners. The company deliberately misleads its stakeholders by reporting false financial information, and the managers know that it is false.

It is difficult for CPA auditors to detect accounting fraud that is instigated and implemented by high-level managers, especially if it is cleverly concealed and involves conspiracy among managers and other parties to the fraud. (Chapter 21 discusses financial statement audits by CPAs.) Auditors are highly skilled professionals, and the failure rate of auditors to discover fraud has been relatively low. However, in some cases CPAs, including those with the Big Four international CPA firms, were negligent in carrying out their audit procedures or they were complicit with management. The CPA firm deserved to be sued—and were!

The bottom line is that there is a small risk that the financial statements you depend on are, in fact, false and seriously misleading. You would have legal recourse against the company's executives and its CPA auditors once the fraud is found out, but this is not a happy situation. Almost certainly you'd end up losing money, even after recovering some of your losses through legal action.

Is It Worth Your Time to Compute Financial Statement Ratios?

We doubt it. The conventional wisdom is that by diligent reading of financial statements you will discover under- or overvalued securities. However, the evidence doesn't support this premise. Market prices reflect all publicly available information about a business, including the information in its latest quarterly and annual financial reports. (Insiders may be privy to information about coming events and take advantage of their position to make trades before the information becomes public knowledge.)

Computing financial statement ratios can be a valuable learning experience. But don't expect to find out something that the market doesn't already know. It's unlikely that you will find a nugget of information that has been overlooked by everyone else. Forget it; it's not worth your time as an investor. The same time would be better spent keeping up with current business and economic developments reported in the financial press.

Why Read Financial Statements, Then, If You Won't Find Information That Has Been Overlooked by Others?

You should know what you are getting into. Does the company have a lot of debt and a heavy interest load to carry? For that matter, is the company in bankruptcy or in a debt workout situation? Has the company had a consistent earnings record over the past 5 to 10 years, or has its profit ridden a roller coaster over this time? Has the company consistently paid cash dividends for many years? Has the company suffered a major loss recently? Has the company given its executives stock options on a large number of shares? Has the company issued more than one class of stock shares?

You would obviously inspect a house before getting serious about buying it, to see if it is in good condition and whether it has two stories, three or more bedrooms, a basement, a good general appearance, and so on. Likewise, you should know the "financial architecture" of a business before investing your capital in its securities. Financial statements serve this getting-acquainted purpose very well, as long as you know what to look for.

One basic stock investment strategy is to search through financial reports or financial statement data on websites, to find corporations that meet certain filtering criteria—for example, whose market values are less than their book values, or whose cash and cash equivalent per share are more than a certain percent of their current market value. Whether these stocks end up beating the market is another matter. In any case, financial statements can be culled through to find whatever types of companies you are looking for.

The Financial Statements and Footnotes of Large Public Companies Would Take Several Hours to Read Carefully. What's the Alternative?

Large businesses produce large financial reports! Their financial statements generally are long, complex, and include several pages of densely written footnotes. Quite literally it would take you several hours, or even longer, to conscientiously read every item in all the financial statements of a company, and every sentence in every footnote. Also, don't forget the auditor's report (also written in technical language), the letter from the CEO to shareholders, and the statement by top management concerning its responsibility for internal controls designed to prevent fraudulent financial reporting. We have to wonder whether professional stock analysts and investment managers have the time to read through the entire financial reports of all the companies they follow and invest in. Maybe they delegate this job to their subordinates, in which case we hope *they* have the time and understand financial statements.

Being aware of how long it takes to read their financial reports cover to cover, most public companies provide *condensed annual financial statements* to their shareholders. The actual financial statements of the business are collapsed into brief summaries of their income statement, balance sheet, and statement of cash flows. These condensed financial statements are *not* accompanied by footnotes and often do not refer to the CPA auditor's report.

If you don't have time to delve into the actual financial statements and footnotes of a company, you should at least read its condensed financial statements. This is better than nothing. By the way, most not-for-profit organizations (such as AARP, for example) issue condensed financial statements to their members. In some situations we still want to read the actual financial statements. As we start reading them we know we're in for a long night that only an accounting professor could love.

Is There Any One Basic Litmus Test for a Quick Gauge of a Company's Financial Performance?

We suggest that you compute the percent increase (or decrease) in sales revenue this year compared with last year, and use this percent as the baseline for testing changes in bottom-line profit (net income) as well as the changes in the major operating assets of the business. Assume sales revenue increased 10 percent over last year. Did profit increase 10 percent? Did accounts receivable, inventory, and long-term operating assets increase about 10 percent?

This is no more than a so-called quick-and-dirty method, but it does point out major disparities. For instance, suppose inventory jumped 50 percent even though sales revenue increased only 10 percent. This may signal a major management mistake; the over-stock of inventory might lead to write-downs later. Management does not usually comment on such disparities in financial reports. You'll have to find them yourself—hopefully not many.

Do Financial Statements Report the Truth, the Whole Truth, and Nothing but the Truth?

There are really two questions here. One question concerns how truthful is profit accounting, which depends on the company's choice of accounting methods from the menu of generally accepted alternatives and how faithfully the methods are applied year in and year out. The other question concerns how honest and forthright are the disclosures in the company's financial report.

Revenue and expenses should be recorded honestly and consistently according to the accounting methods adopted by the business. In other words, once accounting choices have been made, the business should apply the methods and let the chips fall where they may. However, there is convincing evidence that managers of public companies occasionally, if not regularly, intervene and take certain actions to affect the amounts recorded in sales revenue and expenses. They do this to produce more favorable results than would otherwise happen—something akin to the "thumb on the scale" trick. (We discuss massaging the numbers in Chapter 20.)

Manipulating the accounting numbers is done to smooth reported earnings, to balance out unwanted perturbations and oscillations in annual earnings. Investors in public companies seem to prefer a nice steady trend of earnings instead of unpredictable fluctuations, and managers oblige. So, be warned that annual earnings probably are smoothed to some extent.

Disclosure in financial reports is another matter. Both public and private companies are generally reluctant to lay bare all the facts of interest to their lenders and shareholders. Bad news is usually suppressed or at least deemphasized as long as possible. Clearly, there is a lack of candor and frank discussion in many financial reports. Few companies are willing to wash their dirty linen in public by making full disclosure of their mistakes and difficulties in their financial reports. One notable exception to this reluctance to share bad news is the annual letter to the stockholders by Warren Buffett, chairman of Berkshire Hathaway. He lays both good news and bad news on the line, and admits his mistakes.

Public companies include a *management discussion and analysis* (MD&A) section in their annual financial reports. Usually this is a fairly sanitized version of what happened during the year. The history of financial reporting disclosure practices, unfortunately, makes clear that until standard-setting authorities force specific disclosure standards on companies, few will make such disclosures voluntarily.

Some years ago the disclosure of employee pension and retirement costs went through this pattern of inadequate reporting until, finally, the standard-setting body in the United States stepped in and required fuller disclosure. Recalls of unsafe products, pending lawsuits, and top management compensation are examples of reluctant reporting. Here is a historical example: Until the standard was adopted in 1987, companies did not report a statement of cash flows, even though this information had been asked for by security analysts since the 1950s!

The masthead of the *New York Times* boasts, "All the News That's Fit to Print." Don't expect this in companies' financial reports, however.

Does Its Financial Report Explain the Basic Profit-Making Strategy of the Business?

Not really. In an ideal world, we would argue, a financial report should not merely report how much profit (net income) was earned by the business and the amounts of revenue and expenses that generated this profit. The financial report should also provide a profit road map, or an earnings blueprint of the business. The financial report should clarify the so-called business model of the company. Financial report readers should be told the basic profit-making strategy of the business, including its most critical profit-making success factors.

In their annual financial reports, publicly owned corporations are required to disclose their sales revenue and operating expenses by major segments (lines of business). Segmenting a business into its major lines of sales provides information about which major product lines are more profitable than others. However, segments are conglomerate totals that span many different products. Segment disclosure was certainly a step in the right direction. For example, the breakdown between domestic versus international sales revenue and operating profit is important for many businesses.

Businesses are careful not to divulge too much information in their financial reports about their profit margins on specific products (and services). For example, Apple does not reveal the gross margin it makes on sales of its iPhone versus its iPad. Profit margin information is treated as confidential, and is kept away from competitors and from investors in the business as well. The income statement in an external financial report is not the profit report you would see if you were the CEO of the business.

Does the Market Price of a Public Company's Stock Shares Depend Directly and Only on the Information Reported in Its Financial Statements?

Well, you know the answer to this question, don't you? The market price of a public company's stock shares depends on many factors, although the information reported in its financial statements is the main point of reference. We include this question only to remind you that a public company's financial statements are only one source—albeit one of the most important sources—of the information that investors use to make their buy, hold, and sell decisions.

Does the Balance Sheet of a Private Business Tell the Market Value of the Business?

No. The balance sheet of a private business does not report what the market value of the company would be if the business as a whole were on the auction block. The dollar amounts you see in a balance sheet are the results of its actual transactions and operations. The net income (bottom-line profit) reported in the annual income statement of a business summarizes its actual sales revenue for the year minus its actual expenses for the period. Likewise, the cash flows reported by the business are the actual amounts of cash flowing through the business during the year. In short, financial statements are prepared on a "look-back" or historical basis, not on a "look-ahead" basis for determining the market value of the business.

Until there is a serious buyer, it's anyone's guess how much a private business is worth. A buyer may be willing to pay much more than the book value of its owners' equity that is reported in its most recent balance sheet. The market value depends on many factors, as you probably know. Even Warren Buffett, the sage investor who is CEO of Berkshire Hathaway, admits that he has made mistakes in amounts he paid for some businesses in his annual letter to stockholders (which you can read on the company's website).

Generally, the market value of a private business depends mainly on its profit-making ability projected into the future. A buyer may be willing to pay 10 times the annual net income of a privately held business. But we would quickly add that other factors could also play a dominant role in setting the market value of a private business.

Also, we should mention that earnings-based values are quite different from liquidation-based values for a business. Suppose a company is in bankruptcy proceedings or in a troubled debt workout situation. In this unhappy position, the claims of its debt securities and other liabilities dominate the value of its stock shares and owners' equity. Indeed, the company's stock shares may have zero value in such cases.

Do Books on Investing and Personal Finance Refer to Financial Statements?

It may come as a surprise to you, but generally these books say little to nothing about financial statements. The books make little effort to explain even the basics of financial statements, or ignore financial statements altogether. Don't get us wrong. There are many excellent books on investing and personal finance, and we have read quite a few of them.

We feel obligated to warn you that some of the most popular of these books contain little practical advice that you can actually use. Some of these books explain, for example, that if you save 10 percent of your annual income and invest it wisely, then after 40 years you will have a nice sum of money. As John's grandkids would say: duh! In any case, we are perplexed that so few of the good investing and personal finance books discuss financial statements in any depth, or they ignore financial statements altogether.

Financial statements are the essential wellspring of information for business investors and lenders. Indeed, where else do you get this vital information? Not having this financial information would be like trying to find your destination in a city without street signs and traffic signals.

A Very Short Summary

You can generally rely on audited financial statements, although the rash of accounting frauds during over the past two or three decades that CPA auditors failed to discover shook our confidence somewhat. Overall, the percent of fraudulent financial reports among all public businesses is low (but not zero). In any case, investors don't really have an alternative source of financial information about a business other than its financial statements. Accounting fraud, unfortunately, is an unavoidable risk of investing.

You might think twice before investing much time in analyzing the financial statements of corporations whose securities are publicly traded—because thousands of other investors have done the same analysis and the chance of you finding out something that no one else has yet discovered is virtually nil. For a quick benchmark test, though, you might compare the percent change in the company's sales revenue over past year with the percent changes in its net income and operating assets. Major disparities are worth a look.

Reading financial statements is the best way to get acquainted with the financial structure of a business that you're thinking of investing in. Don't worry too much about the accounting methods used by public companies. For privately owned companies, however, you should keep an eye on the major accounting policies of the business and how these accounting methods affect reported earnings and asset values.

Disclosure in financial statements leaves a lot to be desired. Don't look for a road map of the profit strategy of a business in its financial reports. Keep in mind that the total value of a business is not to be found in its balance sheet. Until an actual buyer of a business makes a serious offer, there is no particular reason to determine the value of the business as a going concern. Value depends mainly on the past earnings record of the business as forecast into the future.

The main message of this chapter is to be prudent and careful in making decisions based on financial statements. Many investors and managers don't seem to be aware of the limitations of financial statements. Used intelligently, financial reports are the indispensable starting point for making investment and lending decisions. We hope this book helps you make better decisions. Good luck, and be careful out there.

23

SMALL BUSINESS FINANCIAL REPORTING

In the United States today there are, quite literally, millions of small businesses. In comparison, there are about 5,000 public companies whose stocks are traded on securities markets. And there are thousands of large private companies whose ownership shares are not traded in a public marketplace.

Regardless of size, all businesses need effective accounting systems for conducting operations, for complying with tax laws, and for providing essential financial information to their managers (especially profit or loss, financial condition, and cash flows). Then there is the fourth function of accounting—preparing the *external financial reports* of the business to its lenders and outside investors who don't participate in managing the business.

The financial statements of a business depend on the completeness and accuracy of its accounting records, of course, and on the profit accounting methods the business uses. In Chapter 3 we explain the assets and liabilities used in recording revenue and expenses. Profit accounting drives a large portion of the assets and liabilities reported in the balance sheet. Suppose a company's profit accounting methods are wrong. Then the values reported by the company for some of its assets and liabilities would be inaccurate. Both its income statement and balance sheet would have errors.

Up to the time of revising this book all businesses, large and small, private and public, were subject to the same accounting and financial reporting standards. In actual practice, however, small businesses were cut a lot of slack. No one got too excited if a small business deviated from the standards (well, within limits). Nevertheless, small businesses were supposed to follow the same rules. But this "one-size-fits-all" approach is changing. Recently the accounting profession has taken steps to differentiate the standards for public and private businesses, and for small and large businesses.

Different Standards for Different Businesses

Public companies in the United States are required to use *generally accepted accounting principles*, or GAAP. The codification of these standards runs more than 2,000 pages. Public companies are required to have annual audits of their financial reports by an independent CPA firm to test whether the business is complying with GAAP, or we should say *American* GAAP. In the near future international accounting standards probably will come into effect—although it's difficult to predict when and to what extent the "internationalization" of accounting standards for public companies will take place. It's still a work in progress at the time of revising this book. The Securities and Exchange Commission has not yet approved the adoption of international standards by U.S. companies.

As far as we can tell, large private companies use GAAP and most have annual audits by independent CPAs. Having said this, we should quickly mention that in 2013 the accounting profession established the Private Company Council (PCC), which provides a mechanism to allow exceptions and modifications to GAAP for private companies. Therefore, in the future there will be a private company version of GAAP.

One impetus behind permitting different accounting standards for private companies is to relieve them of the burden of applying provisions in GAAP that have questionable informational value to the users of private company financial reports. The idea is to allow private companies to issue financial reports that are easier to read and to understand. Undoubtedly exceptions and modifications will be enacted. In fact, the PCC is off to a running start. We cannot hazard a guess regarding how different private company accounting standards will deviate from GAAP for public companies.

Small businesses, it is fair to say, never have been overly concerned about sticking tightly to GAAP. For one thing many provisions of GAAP do not apply to small businesses. Also, their accountants were too busy to take the time to keep up with the many changes in GAAP. Small business accounting procedures are guided more by expediency than by close adherence to good accounting theory. The result is that small businesses take many accounting shortcuts.

Here's a simple example of an expedient accounting shortcut. The amount of a prepaid expense should be allocated over the months benefited by the cost (e.g., prepaid insurance premiums). Instead, the small business may simply record the entire cost to expense when paid. You might refer to Chapter 3, which can be used as a checklist of profit accounting questions that small businesses must decide. Instead of the preferred accrual basis accounting methods we explain in Chapter 3, many small businesses use the simpler cash basis for some of their expenses.

As a general rule the larger a small business, the better qualified is its accounting personnel and the more often the business uses an outside CPA to advise the business on accounting and financial reporting issues. A business with $50 million annual sales revenue is more likely to use better accounting methods and issue better financial reports than a small business with $5 million annual sales revenue. As you move down the scale to smaller businesses our experience is that you find a bigger percent of troublesome financial reports.

In June 2013 the American Institute of Certified Public Accountants (AICPA) issued a *financial reporting framework for small- and medium-size entities*. Here's the description of this new framework (taken from an online announcement of an AICPA webcast explaining the new framework):

> The Financial Reporting Framework for Small- and Medium-Sized Entities (FRF for SMEs) is the tool to prepare streamlined, relevant financial statements for privately held small- and medium-sized entities that do not need GAAP-compliant reports. With this framework financial statements can be generated that clearly and concisely report what a business owns, what it owes and its cash flow. Lenders and others can clearly and quickly understand key measures and whether a business is credit-worthy. The FRF for SMEs is the CPA profession's answer to the financial reporting needs of small- and medium-sized companies.

The framework runs about 200 pages and is designed as guidance for the accountants of small- and medium-size businesses. You could call the new framework an *easing* away from the complex and technical GAAP standards. The new framework allows for deviations from GAAP. We suspect that one reason for releasing the new framework was the substandard accounting and financial reporting practices of small- and medium-size businesses.

Hopefully the new framework will improve the overall accounting and financial reporting of small- and medium-size businesses. However, we doubt that the new framework will have widespread effect. Only time will tell. The new framework should have its biggest impact on larger small businesses. The larger a business, the more likely it employs a staff of qualified accountants. And, the more likely its lenders and individual investors demand that the business toe the line in its profit accounting and financial reporting.

Reading a Small Business Financial Report

In this section we identify problems you will likely encounter in reading the financial report of a small business. We take the point of view of the outside readers of the financial report, namely the company's primary lender(s) and the individual investors in the business. The financial report does circulate beyond this narrow group of readers. It goes without saying that its managers should get the financial information they need to run their business. See our *Small Business Financial Management Kit for Dummies* (Tracy and Tracy, 2007, John Wiley & Sons).

A small business that has only one owner/manager may not regularly prepare external financial reports—although, its bank or other lender may demand a financial report. In the following discussion we assume that the small business has prepared a financial report that summarizes the company's financial activity and condition for the most recent period. As we explain early in the book, these summaries consist of three core financial statements—the income statement, the balance sheet, and the statement of cash flows.

We cannot list every possible problem you might encounter in reading a small business financial report. Hopefully you will not bump into these problems. But you should be aware of the following potential problems.

- **Are you reading a financial report?** The information you get from the small business may not actually be an external financial report. What you receive could be a copy of the financial schedules and summaries that the manager of the business uses.

In other words, what you have in your hands may not be an external financial report as such. The manager may be sharing information with you that he or she uses, without preparing a separate financial report.

- **Are second-best accounting methods being used?** The small business may use some accounting methods that are not entirely kosher and strictly according to the rulebook. Generally, these are accounting shortcuts and are not deliberate manipulations of profit and financial condition. On the other hand, the small business could be massaging the numbers. A small business might even cook its books and commit accounting fraud. (Refer to Chapter 20 for more information.)

- **Was an independent CPA involved in preparing the financial report?** Few small businesses have an annual audit of their financial statements by an independent CPA. The cost would be too high. On the other hand, a small business might hire a CPA to review its accounting methods and financial report, or a CPA might have assisted in the compilation of the financial report. The involvement of a CPA adds credibility to the financial report.

- **Which accounting and financial reporting standards are used?** One advantage of an audit by an independent CPA is that the auditor states clearly which accounting and reporting standards are used by the business. It would be helpful if the small business would identify the accounting and reporting

Small business financial reporting **213**

standards used to prepare the financial report. But, don't expect to see this in a small business financial report.

- **Is there adequate disclosure?** Most small businesses put a high premium on confidentiality and privacy—so, they are reluctant to disclose information beyond what is absolutely essential in their financial statements. For that matter big businesses are also reluctant to divulge more financial information than they have to.

- **Is the company's accountant qualified?** The small business may not employ a qualified accountant (not necessarily a CPA, but one that has sufficient education and experience). Accounting computer software can help in pulling together the financial statements of a small business. But a qualified accountant is needed as well.

- **Is a statement of cash flows included?** The financial report may not include a statement of cash flows. This omission is a big red flag! This financial statement has been required for more than a quarter of a century. The absence of the cash flow statement may signal that the company's accountant does not know how to prepare this financial statement or is unaware that it is a required financial statement.

- **Sales skimming?** The owner/manager of the small business could be *sales skimming*. As you may know, this term refers to diverting some of the company's revenue directly into the manager's pocket. The amount skimmed is not recorded in the books of the company, and is not included in sales revenue in the income statement. Bottom-line profit is reduced by the amount of revenue skimmed during the year.

- **Are personal expenses run through the business?** The company may be used to pay personal and family expenses of the owner/manager of the small business. You could argue that this is just an additional form of compensation to the manager. But doing this may violate agreements entered into by the business with other persons, and it could border on income tax evasion.

- **Are there related party transactions?** Transactions with related parties may not be disclosed in the small business report. For example, the owner/manager of the small business may also own a real estate investment business, which leases space to the small business. Because of the common ownership of both companies setting the rent is not an arm's-length transaction. The rent could be set deliberately higher or lower than the going rate, in order to raise or lower the expenses of the small business.

Summing up, small business lenders and outside investors should be cautious and somewhat skeptical when reading the financial report of a small business. They should be on the lookout for the problems we discuss above. As the saying goes, "it is what it is." Although not perfect, the reporting of financial information by small businesses to their lenders and individual investors is better than no financial reporting at all. Lenders and investors can ask questions and request more information from the business—and they may have to.

ABOUT THE AUTHORS

John A. Tracy (Boulder, Colorado) is professor of accounting, emeritus, at the University of Colorado in Boulder. Before his 35-year tenure at Boulder, he was on the business faculty for four years at the University of California, Berkeley. Early in his career he was a staff accountant with Ernst & Young. John is the author of several books on accounting and finance, including *Accounting For Dummies*, *Accounting Workbook For Dummies*, *The Fast Forward MBA in Finance*, and *Cash Flow For Dummies* and *Small Business Financial Management Kit For Dummies* with his son Tage C. Tracy. John received his BSC degree from Creighton University. He earned his MBA and PhD degrees at the University of Wisconsin in Madison. He is a CPA (inactive status) in Colorado.

Tage C. Tracy (Poway/San Diego, California) has operated TMK & Associates (a niche consulting service firm) since 1993. TMK & Associates has focused on providing executive level accounting, financial, and strategic business planning management, training, and consultative services to businesses of all shapes, sizes, and forms (in the role of an interim/part-time CFO, a senior financial/accounting executive, and/or by providing training and seminar programs to broader audiences).

Including *The Comprehensive Guide to How to Read a Financial Report*, Tage has now co-authored a total of four books with his father John A. Tracy, including *Cash Flow For Dummies*, *Small Business Financial Management Kit For Dummies*, and *How to Manage Profit and Cash Flow*.

Tage received his baccalaureate in accounting in 1985 from the University of Colorado at Boulder with honors. Tage began his career with Coopers & Lybrand (now merged into PricewaterhouseCoopers) and obtained his CPA certificate in the state of Colorado in 1987 (now inactive).

http://site.tracyandtracybooks.com/

INDEX